IFLA Publications 97

The Public Library Service

IFLA/UNESCO Guidelines
for Development

Prepared by a working group chaired by Philip Gill
on behalf of the Section of Public Libraries

K · G · Saur   München 2001

IFLA Publications
edited by Carol Henry

Recommended catalogue entry:

The Public library service: IFLA/UNESCO guidelines for development /
[International Federation of Library Associations and Institutions].
Ed. for the Section of Public Libraries by Philip Gill et. al. -
München : Saur, 2001, XVI, 116 p. 21 cm
  (IFLA publications ; 97)
  ISBN 3-598-21827-3

Die Deutsche Bibliothek - CIP-Einheitsaufnahme

The public library service : IFLA/UNESCO guidelines for development /
[International Federation of Library Associations and Institutions].
Prepared by a working group chaired by Philip Gill on behalf of the Section of Public Libraries. -
München : Saur, 2001
  (IFLA publications ; 97)
  ISBN 3-598-21827-3

Printed on acid-free paper
The paper used in this publication meets the minimum requirements of American National
Standard for Information Sciences – Permanence of Paper for Printed Library Materials,
ANSI Z39.48.1984.

Printed / Bound by Strauss Offsetdruck, Mörlenbach

ISBN 3-598-21827-3
ISSN 0344-6891 (IFLA Publications)

Contents

Preface

This publication replaces *Guidelines for public libraries* published in 1986. It has been drafted by a working group made up of members of the Committee of the IFLA Section of Public Libraries. The members of the working group were:

Philip Gill (United Kingdom), Chair
Barbara Clubb (Canada)
Ilona Glashoff (Germany)
Kerstin Hassner (Sweden)
Nerses Hayrapetian (Armenia)
Robert Pestell (Australia).

Before drafting began, the contents of the proposed publication were discussed at a two-day seminar at Noordwijk, Netherlands held in August 1998. We are grateful to UNESCO for their support for this event. Working drafts have been presented and debated at the IFLA Conferences in Amsterdam (1998), Bangkok (1999) and Jerusalem (2000). It has also been considered in detail by the IFLA Committee of the Section of Public Libraries, the Coordinating Board of IFLA Division 3 Libraries Serving the General Public and representatives of IFLA's Professional Board.

The contributions at the Noordwijk seminar, at the IFLA Conferences and by those to whom the drafts have been sent for consultation, have been invaluable. We are grateful to all those who have commented on the work as it has progressed and to those who have provided practical examples to illustrate the text. We are also grateful to the Assistant Director (Lifelong Learning), Buckinghamshire County Council, England for permission to reproduce their Library Service Customer Charter.

The interest shown in this publication as it has been in preparation is evidence of the demand for guidelines for public libraries that reflect the changed information world in which they now operate. We trust that these guidelines will be relevant to public libraries at varying stages of development in the early years of the 21st century and can help librarians to meet the exciting challenges they now face. It is in that belief that we offer this publication to all those who are involved in the development of public libraries throughout the world.

Introduction

In 1994 the third version of the *IFLA/UNESCO Public Library Manifesto* was published. It rapidly became recognized as an important statement of the fundamental principles of the public library service. It has been translated into over twenty languages and become an influential document in public library development (see Appendix 1) . It also became apparent that there was a need and a demand for a more detailed statement of practical guidelines and standards that librarians and policy-makers could use in developing public library services. The committee of the IFLA Section of Public Libraries decided to prepare new guidelines and appointed a group of six of its members to carry out the drafting.

In 1973 IFLA published *Standards for public libraries*, reissued with slight revisions in 1977. In 1986 this was replaced by *Guidelines for public libraries*. Both these publications have been overtaken by the dramatic developments in information technology that have taken place in the last few years. As their titles suggest they represented two different approaches to providing practical guidance to librarians. The introduction to the 1973 *Standards* states:

> Separate standards were not considered desirable, since the general objectives in all countries were the same, the modifying factor being the pace at which development could take place.

The 1973 version therefore provides a range of quantitative standards including the size of collections, size of administrative units, opening hours, staffing levels and building standards.

Those drafting the 1986 *Guidelines* took a different view:

When needs and resources vary so widely there can be no common standards for services . . . We are offering not rules but advice, based on experience drawn from many different countries and capable of general application . . . Recommendations as to desirable levels of provision, based on past experience in quite different circumstances, are bound to be unreliable and misleading.

Statistics of public libraries in different countries were provided in an appendix against which librarians could measure their own service.

In preparing this new edition many issues were raised and addressed but perhaps the three key questions were:

- Should the final document include both guidelines and quantitative standards or be limited just to guidelines?
- Would it be possible to prepare a version that could be of practical use to librarians in countries with public library services at different stages of development and with very different levels of available resources?
- Is it possible to make recommendations on the use of information and communications technology in public libraries when there are such great variations in its availability and in the resources to provide and support it?

In order to get a view on these and other issues, a seminar was held in Noordwijk, Netherlands in August 1998 to discuss the content of the new edition and the form that it should take. The seminar was attended by 22 librarians from 21 countries in different parts of the world and from public libraries at different stages of development and with varying levels of resources. The conclusions reached at the end of that stimulating event have informed the work of the group carrying out the revision.

The Noordwijk delegates strongly supported the view that the new publication should include some practical standards and not be confined to guidelines and recommendations. It became apparent that, though many people were aware of the 1973 *Standards* and still used them to a certain extent, the 1986 *Guidelines* had not made the same practical impact. Though fully aware of the wide variety of social and economic circumstances within which public libraries in different countries operate the drafting group decided that, if this new edition was to have practical value, it should include some recommended standards.

The decision to include standards highlights the importance of the second question: can a set of standards and guidelines have universal relevance? As each draft has been produced it has been sent to the Noordwijk delegates, and to a number of other people who have shown interest in the project, for their reaction. Meetings have been held on the project at the IFLA conferences in Amsterdam (1998), Bangkok (1999) and Jerusalem (2000). This consultative process has been an invaluable element of the project and has revealed both the strength of the public library movement world-wide and the similarities and differences in public libraries in different countries and societies.

Despite the variations in levels of service and in funds to support and develop them, it was decided that it would not be fruitful to attempt to prepare a new edition which was aimed at one group of public libraries, for example those in the 'developed' or the 'developing' world. Such categorization is misleading as the level and range of services and their effectiveness is not necessarily based on the available resources. Libraries in any country and at any stage of development are capable of improvement and all will have both strengths and weaknesses. It was decided, therefore, to produce a set of guidelines and standards that could be relevant to any public library at some point in its development. We recognize the problem of meeting standards when reliable population figures are not available and have suggested alternative approaches. We recommend that the more detailed guidelines produced by specialist sections of IFLA are also used. Where public libraries cannot meet all the standards and recommendations immediately, it is hoped that they will provide a target at which to aim. This publication is aimed primarily at librarians, for them to use in fighting for improved library services.

We have also included some examples of service provision from around the world. These are not intended to be comprehensive or necessarily the most outstanding instances of service provision. They are intended to illustrate the text with some snapshots of what is happening in public libraries in different countries and to provide a glimpse of imaginative solutions to specific challenges. We realize that these are very selective and many more examples could be used that would be equally relevant. They do demonstrate what is being done throughout the world to match the public library service to the needs of its users in a local context. We have also included website addresses for some of the initiatives, to provide access to more detailed information about them.

In the last few years the rapid and very exciting developments in information technology have revolutionized the way in which information is collected, displayed and accessed. The synergy between information and communications technology is allowing access to information in ways hardly imaginable when the last *Guidelines* were published in 1986. The speed of change has accelerated and continues to do so. There are few sectors of activity not affected and the public library, for which the provision of information is a primary role, is facing the challenge of radical changes in all aspects of its organization and service delivery.

Many public libraries have responded to the challenge of the electronic revolution and taken the opportunity to develop services in new and exciting ways. There is, however, another side to this story. The United Nations Human Development Report 1999, while stating that the Internet is the fastest growing tool of communication ever, revealed that South Asia with 23.5% of the world's population has less than 0.1% of the world's Internet users. A quarter of the countries of the world has less than one telephone for every hundred people. To take advantage of the opportunities information and communications technology present there is a basic need for literacy, computer skills and a reliable telecommunications network. The risk of a growing gap between the information rich and the information poor has never been greater. This gap is not just an issue between countries at different stages of development but also between groups and individuals within countries. The United Nations report says 'Determined efforts are needed to bring developing countries – and poor people every where – into the global conversation.'

Public libraries have an exciting opportunity to help to bring everyone into this global conversation and to bridge what is often called 'the digital divide'. They can achieve this by providing information technology for public access, by teaching basic computer skills and by participating in programmes to combat illiteracy. However, to fulfil the principle of access for all, they must also continue to maintain services that provide information in different ways, for example, through print or the oral tradition.

These are likely to remain of vital importance for the foreseeable future. While becoming the gateway to the electronic information world should be a key objective for the public library, every effort must be made not to close other doors through which knowledge and information can be provided. These factors present public libraries with a major challenge, and their response will determine the continuing viability of the public library service. The recommendations have been framed with these issues in mind.

In the introduction to the 1986 *Guidelines* Arthur Jones wrote

> The working group identified many imperatives: the words 'must' and 'should' occur frequently. Nevertheless this is not a set of rules for designing an ideal library service: it is a tool to help in the development of services which will best meet the needs of your own community. The guidelines will suggest what might be possible, but local conditions will dictate what is feasible, with regard to both services and organisation.

We would echo that statement. The public library is a locally based service meeting the needs of the local community and operating within the context of that community. These guidelines have been framed to provide assistance to librarians in any situation to develop an effective public library service related to the requirements of their local community. In this exciting and complex information world it is important for those in search of knowledge, information and creative experience that they succeed.

Philip Gill

1

The role and purpose of the public library

'The public library, the local gateway to knowledge, provides a basic condition for lifelong learning, independent decision-making and cultural development of the individual and social groups.'

(*IFLA/UNESCO Public Library Manifesto*, 1994)

1.1 Introduction

This chapter is a general statement on the role and purpose of the public library. The key issues are developed in greater detail in later chapters.

1.2 Defining the public library

Public libraries are a world-wide phenomenon. They occur in a variety of societies, in differing cultures and at different stages of development. Although the varied contexts in which they operate inevitably result in differences in the services they provide, and the way those services are delivered, they normally have characteristics in common, which can be defined as follows.

A public library is an organization established, supported and funded by the community, either through local, regional or national government or through some other form of community organization. It provides access to knowledge, information and works of the imagination through a range of resources and services and is equally available to all members of the community regardless of race, nationality, age, gender, religion, language, disability, economic and employment status and educational attainment.

1.3 The purposes of the public library

The primary purposes of the public library are to provide resources and services in a variety of media to meet the needs of individuals and groups for education, information and personal development including recreation and leisure. They have an important role in the development and maintenance of a democratic society by giving the individual access to a wide and varied range of knowledge, ideas and opinions.

1.3.1 Education

'Supporting both individual and self conducted education as well as formal education at all levels.'

(Manifesto)

The need for an agency available to all, which provides access to knowledge in printed and other formats to support formal and informal education, has been the reason for the foundation and maintenance of most public libraries and remains a core purpose for the public library. Throughout their lives people require education either at formal institutions, for example, schools, colleges and universities, or in a less formal context related to their employment and daily life. Learning does not end with the completion of formal education but is, for most people, a lifelong activity. In an increasingly complex society people will need to acquire new skills at various stages of their life. The public library has an important role in assisting this process.

The public library should provide material in the appropriate media to support formal and informal learning processes. It should also help the user to make use of these learning resources effectively as well as providing facilities that enable people to study. The ability to access information and make effective use of it is vital to successful education and, where possible, public libraries should co-operate with other educational organizations in teaching the use of information resources. Where adequate library facilities exist to support formal education the public library should complement them rather than duplicating library provision available elsewhere.

The public library should also actively support literacy campaigns, as literacy is the key to education and knowledge and to the use of libraries and information services. Newly literate people need easy access to appropriate reading materials to maintain and develop their skills.

In some countries the need for educational development is seen to be paramount and the focus of public libraries is to support formal education. There are, however, a variety of ways in which public libraries can support both formal and informal education. How this is achieved will depend on the local context and the level of available resources.

- ▸ In Singapore the stated mission for the public library service is 'to continuously expand this nation's capacity to learn through a national network of libraries and information resource centres providing services and learning opportunities to support the advancement of Singapore'.
- ▸ In South Africa, where many people have inadequate living space and no electricity to enable them to study, public libraries give a high priority to providing the basic facilities, light, tables and chairs.
- ▸ In many countries libraries that fulfil the function of both public and school library are provided. In Trafford, England, three smaller libraries have been integrated into existing facilities. One branch library has been combined with a school library and two are located with leisure facilities.
- ▸ In Bulawayo, Zimbabwe, a weekly mobile library service visits thirty-seven primary schools greatly increasing access to the library service for children in the city.
- ▸ In Amazonas State, Venezuela, where there are no school libraries, rural libraries concentrate on providing support for school students and teachers.
- ▸ In Barcelona province, Spain, some library services give support to distance learning students from the Open University in Catalonia.
- ▸ In the State of Queensland, Australia, public libraries provide homework resources and support to upper primary and secondary school children through organized homework clubs in libraries. Electronic homework support is also available. (**http://netlinks.slq.qld.gov.au**)

1.3.2   Information

'The public library is the local centre of information making all kinds of knowledge and information readily available to its users.'

(Manifesto)

It is a basic human right to be able to have access to and an understanding of information, and there is now more information available than ever before in the world's history. As a public service open to all, the public library has a key role in collecting, organizing and exploiting information, as well as providing access to a wide range of information sources. The public library has a particular responsibility to collect local information and make it readily available. It also acts as a memory of the past by collecting, conserving and providing access to material relating to the history of the community and of individuals. In providing a wide range of information the public library assists the community in informed debate and decision-making on key issues. In collecting and providing information the public library should, wherever possible, co-operate with other agencies to make the best use of available resources.

The rapid growth in the volume of available information and the continuing technological changes, which have radically affected the way information is accessed, have already made a significant effect on public libraries and their services. Information is very important to the development of the individual and of society, and information technology gives considerable power to those able to access and use it. Despite its rapid growth it is not available to the majority of the world's population, and the gap between the information rich and the information poor continues to widen. A vital role for the public library is to bridge that gap by providing public access to the Internet as well as providing information in traditional formats. Public libraries should recognize and exploit the opportunities provided by the exciting developments in information and communications technology. They have the opportunity to become the electronic gateway to the information world.

▶ Sabah State Library, Malaysia, provides electronic corners in its libraries. These are one-stop sources of information and entertainment, which can access the Internet, and a wide variety of CD-ROMS. Public seminars on how to use the Internet are also organized by the library.

▸ Some public libraries in South Africa provide space for information kiosks and telecentres.

▸ Open access Internet points have been established in public libraries in Estonia.

▸ Rural multi-purpose community telecentres have been established in five African countries (Benin, Mali, Mozambique, Tanzania and Uganda) to provide access to modern information and communication tools.

▸ The public library in Sunderland, England, is developing 'electronic village halls', based in a variety of locations, including library buildings, a further education college, a community business centre, and around a community and voluntary network. They provide free access to PCs (personal computers) and the Internet, a wide range of software for adults and children and trained staff who are available to help users.

1.3.3   Personal development

'Providing opportunities for personal creative development.'

(Manifesto)

The opportunity to develop personal creativity and pursue new interests is important to human development. To achieve this, people need access to knowledge and works of the imagination. The public library can provide access, in a variety of different media, to a rich and varied store of knowledge and creative achievement, which individuals cannot acquire on their own behalf. Providing access to major collections of the world's literature and knowledge, including the community's own literature, has been a unique contribution of the public library and is still a vitally important function. Access to works of the imagination and knowledge is an important contribution to personal education and meaningful recreational activity.

The public library can also make a fundamental contribution to daily survival and social and economic development by being directly involved in providing information to people in developing communities; for example, basic life skills, adult basic education and AIDS awareness programmes. In communities with a high illiteracy rate the public library should provide services for non-literates and interpret and translate information where necessary. It should also provide basic user education.

▸ The Rural Audio Libraries of Mali use cassettes to distribute information on hygiene, health, animal husbandry and other topics relevant to people's daily life. These reach 146 villages, and collective listening sessions are organized.

▸ In Bolivia, local libraries are venues for a variety of activities, for example health campaigns, classes in hygiene and nutrition, mother and baby clubs and youth clubs.

▸ Job information centres are located in 13 libraries in the Pioneer Library System, New York State, USA. Job seekers can get information about jobs and use a variety of media to help prepare applications and for interviews. The project has forged links between library staff and the regional Workforce Development System.

▸ A key objective in developing library services in rural areas in Venezuela is to improve the quality of life by providing information on agriculture and animal husbandry and meet the needs of the small farmer with limited resources.

1.3.4   Children and young people

'Creating and strengthening reading habits in children from an early age.'
(*Manifesto*)

The public library should attempt to meet the needs of all groups in the community regardless of age and physical, economic or social circumstances. However, it has a special responsibility to meet the needs of children and young people. If children can be inspired by the excitement of knowledge and by works of the imagination at an early age, they are likely to benefit from these vital elements of personal development throughout their lives, both enriching them and enhancing their contribution to society. Children can also encourage parents and other adults to make use of the library. It is also important that young people who experience difficulty in learning to read should have access to a library to provide them with appropriate material (see Paragraphs 3.4.2 and 3.4.3).

1.3.5 Public libraries and cultural development

An important role of the public library is providing a focus for cultural and artistic development in the community and helping to shape and support the cultural identity of the community. This can be achieved by working in partnership with appropriate local and regional organizations, by providing space for cultural activity, organizing cultural programmmes and by ensuring that cultural interests are represented in the library's materials. The library's contribution should reflect the variety of cultures represented in the community. It should provide materials in the languages spoken and read in the local community, and support cultural traditions.

▸ Librarians working in Amazonas, Venezuela, are trained to act as intermediaries between different cultures as many people living in the rural communities only speak their native language.

1.3.6 The social role of the public library

The public library has an important role as a public space and meeting place. This is particularly important in communities where there are few places for people to meet. It is sometimes called 'the drawing room of the community'.

Use of the library for research and for finding information relating to the user's education and leisure interests, brings people into informal contact with other members of the community. Using the public library can be a positive social experience.

1.4 An agency for change

In carrying out its role in these key areas the public library is acting as an agency for social and personal development and can be a positive agency for change in the community. By providing a wide range of materials to support education and by making information accessible to all, the public library can bring economic and social benefits to individuals and to the community. It contributes to the creation and maintenance of a well-informed and democratic society and helps to empower people in the enrichment and development of their lives and that of the community in which they live.

The public library should be aware of the issues that are being discussed within the community and provide information that will inform that debate.

1.5   Freedom of information

'Collections and services should not be subject to any form of ideological, political or religious censorship, nor commercial pressures.'

(Manifesto)

The public library should be able to represent all ranges of human experience and opinion, free from the risk of censorship. In some countries a Freedom of Information Act will help to ensure these rights are maintained. Librarians and governing bodies should uphold these basic human rights and resist pressure from individuals and groups to limit the material available in the public library.

1.6   Access for all

A fundamental principle of the public library is that its services must be available to all and not directed to one group in the community to the exclusion of others. Provision should be made to ensure services are equally available to minority groups who for some reason are not able to use the mainstream services, for example, linguistic minorities, people with physical and sensory disabilities or those living in remote communities who are unable to reach library buildings. The level of funding, development of services, the design of libraries and their opening hours should all be planned with the concept of universal access as a basic principle (see Chapter 3 'Meeting the needs of the users').

The development of collections should also be based on the principle of access for all and include access to formats appropriate to specific client groups, for example, Braille and talking books for blind people. Information and communications technology should be used to allow access to the library's collections and those of other information sources, both from within the library or from remote sites.

1.7 Local needs

Public libraries are locally based services for the benefit of the local community and should provide community information services. The services and collections they provide should be based on local needs, which should be assessed regularly. Without this discipline the public library will get out of touch with those it is there to serve and will, as a result, not be used to its full potential. Librarians should, therefore, be aware of the changes in society arising from such factors as social and economic development, demographic change, variations in the age structure, levels of education, patterns of employment and the emergence of other educational and cultural providers.

1.8 Local culture

The public library should be a key agency in the local community for the collection, preservation and promotion of local culture in all its diversity. This can be achieved in a variety of ways, for example, the maintenance of local history collections, exhibitions, storytelling, publishing of items of local interest and developing interactive programmes on local themes. Where the oral tradition is an important method of communication the public library should encourage its continuation and development.

▸ In services offered by the Rural Libraries and Resources Development Programme in Zimbabwe, the incorporation of drama, song and dance as part of information transfer is juxtaposed with reading, lending and literacy support.

▸ Village Reading Rooms in Botswana act as centres for storing Setswana literature and promoting the Setswana language and for the promotion of culture where discussion groups, traditional songs, dances and meetings are organized.

▶ Rural libraries in Cajamarca, Peru are involved in the reinstatement and revitalization of the Andean indigenous language base. A project was set up to publish material on the local culture and the resulting Rural Encyclopaedia provides an alternative to school, empowers people and promotes self-education.

▶ In Singapore, an Asian Library Services Unit provides services in the local languages: Chinese, Malay and Tamil.

▶ In Cuba, libraries act as venues for poets and also encourage research into and the conservation of peasant oral traditions.

▶ One objective of the Village Libraries in India is to provide a platform for documenting traditional knowledge. Books written by villagers are published.

1.9   The cultural roots of the public library

It is important to the long-term success of the library that it should be based on the culture, or cultures, of the country or area in which it operates. It is less likely to succeed if the form and structure of the public library are introduced from a country or area with a very different cultural background.

1.10   Libraries without walls

In developing policies to fulfil the role and purpose of the public library the emphasis should be on the services it provides. In meeting the needs of its community the public library will provide a range of services, some of which (for example, large collections of printed material), can be most effectively delivered from a library building. However, there will be many circumstances where it is more effective to provide the service beyond the walls of the library. Examples will vary in different societies but the principle of planning library development from a service rather than a building perspective is important in all public library policy development. The provision of services using information and communications technology also presents exciting opportunities to take library and information services direct to the home and the workplace.

A variety of forms of transport are used to deliver services to sparsely populated areas. The provision of library and information services to people unable to visit a library due to physical or sensory disability or lack of transport, for example, ensures that access to these services is available to all at their home or workplace regardless of their circumstances.

> ▸ The public library service in Chile has developed a variety of mobile services, bookmobiles, book boats, book boxes, backpacks and bicycles. The services offer books and cultural activities for all ages and travel across all terrains. They also serve rest homes, hospitals and prisons.

1.11   Library buildings

Library buildings play an important part in public library provision. They should be designed to reflect the functions of the library service, be accessible to all in the community and be sufficiently flexible to accommodate new and changing services. They should be located close to other community activities, for example, shops and cultural centres. Wherever possible the library should also be available for community use, for example, for meetings and exhibitions and in larger buildings for theatrical, musical, audiovisual and media performances. A well used public library will make a significant contribution to the vitality of an urban area and be an important learning and social centre and meeting place, particularly in scattered rural areas. Librarians should, therefore, ensure that library buildings are used and managed effectively to make the best use of the facilities for the benefit of the whole community.

1.12   Resources

To fulfil its roles satisfactorily the public library must have adequate resources, not just when it is established but also on a continuing basis, to enable it to sustain and develop services that meet the needs of the local community. This means it should provide materials in all formats, up-dated regularly to meet the changing needs of groups and individuals, including newly-published and replacement materials. It should also provide adequate levels of staff with appropriate training and sufficient funds to support whatever methods of service delivery are needed for it to meet its vital role in the community.

2

The legal and financial framework

'The public library is the responsibility of local and national authorities. It must be supported by specific legislation and financed by national and local governments. It has to be an essential component of any long-term strategy for culture, information provision, literacy and education.'

(IFLA/UNESCO Public Library Manifesto, 1994)

2.1 Introduction

Public libraries are a community agency providing access at local level to a range of knowledge and information for the benefit of the individual and society as a whole. In order to maintain the level of service required to fulfil their functions public libraries should be supported by legislation and sustained funding.

2.2 The public library and government

There are many different models of the relationship between public libraries and government. Equally, the laws that govern their activities and funding arrangements are varied and complex. In different countries, provinces, regions, states or municipalities are, either in whole or in part, responsible for library services. As public libraries are a locally based service local government is often the most appropriate place in the government structure for them. However, in some countries public libraries are provided at regional or state level and the national library sometimes has responsibility for providing the public library service. There are instances of two or more levels of government co-operating in the provision of the service.

> ▸ The Estonian Public Libraries Act (1998) details the responsibilities of each level of government. It states that the public library is established by the local government body, and that the county or city library is responsible for the co-ordination of library service, interlibrary loans and book mobiles. The local authority is responsible for employees' wages but the funding of library materials is shared between the local authority and the state.

2.2.1 Alternative structures

In some countries, although the local authority has nominal responsibility for the public library, it does not have the required funds and non-governmental organizations or private foundations undertake the practical operation of the public library services. However, to ensure sustained development and its role in the information network, the public library should be closely related to and funded by the appropriate level of government. The eventual aim should be to bring public libraries into the formal government structure operating under national legislation and with appropriate levels of funding.

> ▸ Argentina has 1600 popular libraries provided by non-governmental organizations or organized communities and regulated by national legislation.

2.2.2 National information policies

In order to make the most effective use of available library and information resources, and take full advantage of the opportunities offered by the development of electronic information sources, many countries are developing national information policies. Public libraries should be a key element in such policies and public librarians should ensure they are fully involved in their development.

2.3 Public library legislation

Public libraries should be based on legislation, which assures their continuance and their place in the government structure. Public library legislation takes various forms. In some countries or regions the legislation is specific to public libraries whereas in others it is part of wider legislation which includes different types of libraries. Public library legislation is also varied in its provisions. It can be simple, allowing the establishment of public libraries but leaving standards of service to the level of government directly responsible for the library, or more complex, with specific detail on what services should be provided and to what standard. Examples of public library legislation are available on the IFLA website (**http://www.ifla. org/V/cdoc/acts.htm**).

Because governmental structures vary so much in different countries the form and detail of public library legislation is also likely to vary significantly. However, legislation governing public libraries should state which level of government is responsible for their provision and how they should be funded. It should also place them in the framework of libraries in the country or region as a whole.

▶ Mexico and Venezuela have specific public library legislation whereas in Colombia and Brazil legislation on information services includes references to public libraries.

▶ The Finnish Library Act (1998) stipulates that the public library should be provided by the municipality, either independently or in co-operation with other public libraries, that public libraries should co-operate with other types of library and that the municipality should evaluate the library and information services that it provides (see Appendix 2).

▶ The Constitution of the Republic of South Africa 1996 provides the constitutional framework for the provision of library and information services in South Africa. It lists 'libraries other than national libraries' as an area of exclusive provincial legislative competence. It is, therefore, a provincial responsibility to develop the legislative framework in which library and information services can be provided.

▶ In Armenia, local authorities have responsibility for the financing and maintenance of public libraries. The Law on Local Self-Government

(1996) defines their obligations for maintaining and developing public libraries.

▸ In the Russian Federation, there are two laws relating to libraries at federal level, the Library Act and the Legal Deposit Copy Act. They are not concerned solely with public libraries though most of the Library Act is devoted to them.

▸ The Italian Constitution gives Regions the control of public libraries established by municipalities and provinces. Some Regions have issued Library Acts in order to regulate co-operation between libraries and other information, documentation, cultural and educational agencies and to set quality standards.

▸ Guidelines on library legislation and policy in Europe have been issued by the Council of Europe and EBLIDA.

2.3.1 Related legislation

Public libraries are subject to a range of legislation apart from the specific legislation relating to them. This can include legislation on financial management, data protection, health and safety and staff conditions and there will be many other examples. Library managers should be aware of all legislation affecting the operation of the public library.

They should also be aware of global trade negotiations, which can result in policies and agreements, which could have a serious impact on public libraries. In such cases librarians should take every opportunity to bring the effect of such policies on public libraries to the notice of the public and politicians.

2.3.2 Copyright

Copyright legislation, especially that relating to electronic publications, is of particular importance to public libraries. It is constantly subject to amendment and review and librarians should keep up-to-date with the legislation in relation to all media. Librarians should promote and support copyright legislation, which achieves an equitable balance between the rights of creators and the needs of users.

▸ In the Czech Republic the library association SKIP, acting on its own initiative, participated in the preparation of copyright legislation. After discussions with the Ministry of Culture and the Cultural Committee of the Czech parliament, changes beneficial to libraries were introduced.

2.3.3   Public lending right

In some countries, public lending right legislation has been introduced which provides a payment to authors and others involved in the creation of a book, related to its provision in, and loan from, public libraries. It is important that funds for payment of public lending right should not be taken from libraries' funds for the purchase of materials. However, public lending right, if separately funded, does provide support for authors without affecting public libraries' budgets. In some schemes it can also provide useful statistics on the loans of books by specific authors. Librarians should participate in the development of public lending right schemes to ensure they are not financed from library budgets.

▸ The Danish government provides funds for Public Lending Right payments, which go to Danish authors, translators, artists, photographers and composers who contribute to a printed work. This is defined as cultural support (**http://www.bs.dk**).

2.4   Funding

Adequate levels of funding are crucial to the success of a public library in fulfilling its roles. Without suitable levels of funding over the long-term it is impossible to develop policies for service provision and make the most effective use of available resources. This can be seen in number of examples: a new library building without adequate funds to maintain it, collections of new books with no money for their replacement and computer systems without funds to maintain and update them. Funding is required not only when a public library is established, but should also be sustained on an assured and regular basis.

2.4.1   Priorities

A public library and the services it provides is a long-term investment on behalf of the community and should be funded appropriately. It is recognized that even in the wealthiest of societies it may not be possible to provide appropriate levels of funding for every service requirement. It is vitally important, therefore, that service development should be conducted on a planned basis with clear priorities. This process is necessary whatever level of funding is available to the library service. To determine strategic planning and the maintenance of agreed priorities, written policy statements should be developed for services. They should be reviewed at regular intervals and revised where necessary.

2.4.2   Partnership

No public library, however large and well funded, can meet all the needs of its users on its own. Participation in partnerships and networks with other libraries and related organizations, and the provision of access to other sources of information, enables the public library to satisfy the information needs of its users by increasing the range of available resources.

2.4.3   Sources of funding

A number of sources of funding are used to finance public libraries but the proportions of funding from each source will vary depending on local factors in each country.

The primary sources are:

- taxation at local, regional or central level
- block grants from central, regional or local level.

Secondary sources of income may include:

- donations from funding bodies or private individuals

- revenue from commercial activities, e.g., publishing, book sales, sale of works of art and handicrafts
- revenue from user fees, e.g., fines
- revenue from charges to users for individual services, e.g., photocopying and printing facilities
- sponsorship from external organizations
- lottery funds for specific initiatives.

2.4.4   Charging the user

The *IFLA/UNESCO Public Library Manifesto* states: 'The public library shall in principle be free of charge'. Charging users for services and membership should not be used as a source of revenue for public libraries, as it makes the ability to pay a criterion in determining who can use a public library. This reduces access and therefore breaches the fundamental principle that the public library should be available to all. It is recognized that in some countries subscriptions to join the library or charges for specific services are levied. Such charges inevitably deny access to those unable to afford them. They should be seen as an interim situation and not as a permanent feature of public library funding.

It is common in some countries to ask users to pay a fee or fine when keeping an item after it is due for return to the library. This is sometimes necessary to ensure that items are kept in circulation and not retained for a long time by one user. The fine should not be set at a level that would deter anyone from using the library. Charges are also sometimes levied for personalized services, for example photocopying or use of a printer. These charges should also not be set at a level which will deter the user.

2.4.5   Funding for technology

Public libraries must, whenever possible, make use of the new technologies to improve their services and provide new ones. This means a considerable investment in various kinds of electronic equipment, and a reliance on this equipment for the delivery of services. To continue to perform effectively equipment should be upgraded and replaced. This has significant funding consequences and a plan for the replacement and upgrading of technological equipment should be developed.

2.4.6 External funding

Librarians should be imaginative in seeking external sources of funding for the public library. However, they should not accept funding from any source if, by so doing, the fundamental status of a public library as an agency available to all is compromised. Commercial organizations, for example, may offer funding with conditions which might prejudice the universal nature of the services provided by the public library.

▸ The public library in Tarragona, Spain, gets funding from business enterprises in the city to run a commercial and economic information service.

2.5 The governance of the public library

Public libraries should be governed by a properly established body made up largely of representatives of the local community including those elected either to the local council or to the library board. Library committees and boards should have rules of procedure and their proceedings should be open to the general public. They should meet on a regular basis and publish agenda, minutes, annual reports and financial statements. Normally the governing body will be responsible for matters of policy rather than the day-to-day operation of the library. In all cases the chief librarian should have direct access to the meetings of the governing body of the library and work closely with it. Policy documents should be made available to the public and, where possible, steps should be taken to involve local citizens in the development of the public library.

Public librarians must be fully accountable both to their governing bodies and local citizens for their actions by providing reports, holding public meetings and through consultation. They must also maintain the highest professional standards in carrying out their duties and in advising the governing body. Although the final decisions on policy will be taken by the governing body and the librarian, ways should be sought to involve the local citizens who are the actual or potential library users. The concept of a 'library charter', which identifies and publicizes the level of service the public library provides has been developed in some countries (see Appendix 3 for a sample charter). This establishes a 'contract' between the public library and the users. Library charters have more credibility if they are developed in consultation with users.

2.6 The administration of the public library

Public libraries should be well managed and administered. The administration of a public library should be directed towards improving the quality of service to the users and not as an end in itself. It should be efficient and accountable. To get best results the administrative and management staff of a large public library service should be multidisciplinary, involving staff with specialist skills, for example, librarians, accountants, public relations officers and system managers. It may also be necessary to draw on the expertise of staff of the parent authority or other related organization in certain areas, for example, lawyers, payroll and pensions staff.

2.7 Publicity and promotion

Public libraries operate in an increasingly complex society, which makes many calls on people's time and attention. It is important, therefore, that libraries publicize their presence and the range of services they provide. Publicity ranges from simple techniques, like signs on library buildings stating what they are, and leaflets advertising opening hours and services, to more sophisticated methods like marketing programmes and the use of websites to promote the library's services and activities (see Chapter 6 'The management and marketing of public libraries').

3

Meeting the needs of the users

'The services of the public library are provided on the basis of equality of access for all, regardless of age, race, sex, religion, nationality, language or social status.

To ensure nation wide library coordination and cooperation, legislation and strategic plans must also define and promote a national library network based on agreed standards of service.

The public library network must be designed in relation to national, regional, research and special libraries as well as libraries in schools, colleges and universities.

Services have to be physically accessible to all members of the community. This requires well situated library buildings, good reading and study facilities, as well as relevant technologies and sufficient opening hours convenient to the users. It equally implies out-reach services for those unable to visit the library.

The library services must be adapted to the different needs of communities in rural and urban areas.'

(IFLA/UNESCO Public Library Manifesto, 1994)

3.1 Introduction

To be successful in fulfilling its goals the public library service must be fully accessible to all its potential users. Any limitation of access, whether deliberate or accidental, will reduce the ability of the public library to fully achieve its primary role of meeting the library and information needs of the community it serves. The following are important elements in delivering an effective public library service:

- identifying potential users
- analysing users' needs
- developing services to groups and individuals
- introducing customer care policies
- promoting user education
- co-operating and sharing resources
- developing electronic networks
- ensuring access to services
- providing library buildings.

3.2   Identifying potential users

The public library has to aim to serve all citizens and groups. An individual is never too young or too old to use a library.

The public library has the following potential target groups.

- People at all ages and at all stages of life:
  - children
  - young adults
  - adults.
- Individuals and groups of people with special needs:
  - people from different cultures and ethnic groups including indigenous people
  - people with disabilities, e.g., blind and partially sighted, hearing impaired
  - housebound people
  - institutionally confined people, e.g., in hospitals, prisons.
- Institutions within the wider community network:
  - educational, cultural and voluntary organizations and groups in the community
  - the business community
  - the governing body of the parent organization, e.g., local authority.

As resources are limited in even the wealthiest society it is not always possible to serve all users to the same level. The library must establish priorities based on an analysis of user needs and related to their access to alternative services.

3.3　Analysing needs within the community

It is important to establish who uses and who does not use the library service. It is also necessary to collect and analyse data that identifies those needs of individuals and groups within the community that can be met by the public library (see Paragraph 6.10 'Management tools').

3.4　Services to users

The public library must provide services based on an analysis of the library and information needs of the local community. In planning services, clear priorities must be established and a strategy be developed for service provision in the medium to long term. Services should be developed for identified target groups and only provided if such groups exist in the local community.

The services of the library should not be subject to any form of ideological, political, religious or commercial pressure. Services must be able to adjust and develop to reflect changes in society, for example, variations in family structures, employment patterns, demographic changes, cultural diversity and methods of communication. They should take account of traditional cultures as well as new technologies, for example, support for oral methods of communication as well as making use of information and communication technology. In some countries the services that the public library must provide are defined in library legislation.

3.4.1　Service provision

Public libraries provide a range of services, both within the library and in the community, to satisfy their users' needs. The library should facilitate access to its services for all, including those who have difficulty reading print. The following services, which should be easily accessible to the user in a variety of formats and media, should be provided:

- loan of books and other media
- provision of books and other materials for use in the library
- information services using print and electronic media
- readers' advisory services including reservation services

- community information services
- user education including support for literacy programmes
- programming and events.

This is not an exhaustive list but an indication of some of the key services of the public library. The range and depth of provision will depend on the size of the library and the community it serves. Every library should aim to be an active participant in one or more networks, which will give the user access to a wide range of material, however small the access point. Service provision should not be confined to the library building but also taken direct to the user where access to the library is not possible. In providing services, both within the library and beyond, use should be made of information and communications technology as well as the printed word. A list of some of the resources the library should provide is detailed in Paragraph 4.3.1.

3.4.2 Services to children

By providing a wide range of materials and activities, public libraries provide an opportunity for children to experience the enjoyment of reading and the excitement of discovering knowledge and works of the imagination. Children and their parents should be taught how to make the best use of a library and how to develop skills in the use of printed and electronic media.

Public libraries have a special responsibility to support the process of learning to read, and to promote books and other media for children. The library must provide special events for children, such as story telling and activities related to the library's services and resources. Children should be encouraged to use the library from an early age as this will make them more likely to remain users in future years. In multilingual countries books and audiovisual materials for children should be available in their mother tongue.

▸ In France, public libraries in many regions are co-operating with Health Services for Children to organize programmes for parents and their children while they are waiting for medical consultation. These are aimed at children from birth to three years old, to encourage parents to read aloud to their children and to visit the public library.

▸ In Bucharest, Rumania, the city library is offering summer pro-grammes, run by volunteers, aimed at children from 11 to 14 whose parents are at work.

▸ In the Netherlands, groups of people over 50 are trained by the pub-lic library to read to children in schools, kindergarten and child care centres.

▸ In the State of Queensland, Australia, a range of activities for children is provided by the public library, including sessions for under fives, their parents and carers, storytelling, class visits, library orientation, read-ing groups, Internet training and homework clubs.

▸ The library service in Johnson County, Kansas, USA, provides 'Books to Grow' kits for pre-school through to first grade. Each kit has a theme and contains five books, one audio-tape, one video-tape and one activity folder.

▸ In Singapore, 41 children's libraries for children under ten have been established since 1992 in co-operation with a local grassroots organ-ization. They have a collection of 10 000 items, full Internet servic-es and a story-telling room. The funding is shared between the Library Board and the local organization.

▸ During and after the war in Croatia a step-by-step reading programme was organized in Zagreb public library to aid the psycho-social recov-ery of children and adolescents through reading and literacy (**http://www.tel.hr/kgz/head.htm**).

▸ A European project, CHILIAS, is using the Internet and world wide web to offer new library services to children. It has set up Infoplanet, a web-site for children. The project aims to promote reading and the book in a multimedia environment (**http://www.stuttgart.de/chilias/**).

3.4.3   Services for young adults

Young people between childhood and adulthood develop as individual members of society with their own culture. Public libraries must understand their needs and provide services to meet them. Materials, including access to electronic information resources, that reflect their interests and culture should be provided. In some cases this will mean acquiring materials that represent youth culture, in a variety of media that are not traditionally part of a library's resources, for example, popular novels, book and television series, music, video tapes, teenage magazines, posters, computer games, graphic novels. It is important to enlist the help of young people in selecting this material to ensure that it reflects their interests. In larger libraries this material, with appropriate furniture, can form a special section of the library. This will help them to feel that the library is for them and help to overcome a feeling of alienation from the library, which is not unusual among this age group. Relevant programmes and talks to young adults should also be provided (see *IFLA guidelines for library services for young adults*).

▸ In Hamburg, Germany, young adults help to select and buy media stock for the young adults' library in a project called EXIT. They select media reflecting their own cultural background and have organized and gained sponsorship for their own Internet café (**http://www.buecherhallen.de/**).

▸ In Queensland, Australia, public library staff receive specialist training in working with young adults. The training covers customer care, programming ideas and how to run teenage advisory groups and homework clubs. In conjunction with local teenagers many libraries have developed youth spaces (**http://www.slq.qld.gov.au/pub/youthspace/index.htm**).

▸ In Singapore a library aimed at people aged 18–35 has been established in the heart of the shopping area. Focus groups helped to define the profile of the collection and design the library.

3.4.4 Services for adults

Adults will have different requirements of an information and library service related to the variety of situations they will encounter in their studies, employment and personal life. These requirements should be analysed and services be developed on the outcome of that analysis. They should include support for:

- lifelong learning
- leisure time interests

- information needs
- community activities
- cultural activity
- recreational reading.

Services meeting these needs should also be available to children and young adults.

3.4.5 Lifelong learning

The public library supports lifelong learning, working with schools and other educational institutions to help students of all ages with their formal education. The challenge of providing educational support provides an opportunity for public libraries to interact and network with teachers and others involved in education. The public library should also provide a range of materials on a variety of topics which will allow people to follow their interests and support their formal and informal education. It should also provide materials to support literacy and the development of basic life skills. In addition the library must provide study facilities for students who have inadequate or no access to these facilities in their homes.

The development in distance learning is having an impact on the public library. Distant learners, studying at home, are likely to make use of their local library as their primary source for material. Many will require access to the Internet which the public library should provide. Public libraries play an increasingly important role within the educational network and should provide space and access to materials to meet this demand.

▸ South Dublin County Library Service, Ireland, provides self-learning facilities for adults, including computer-based learning and audio- and video-based language-learning materials. The aim is to provide a neutral and supportive environment in which individuals can learn at their own pace.

▸ Two libraries in Oklahoma, USA, sponsor discussion groups for new adult readers with grants from the National Endowment for the

Humanities. The group reads one book at a time, usually a classic, and then discusses it with the help of a group facilitator.

3.4.6   Leisure time interests

People need information to support their leisure time interests and meeting this need by a range of resources in a variety of formats is another key role of the public library. Public libraries must be aware of the cultural, social and economic changes in the community and develop services that are sufficiently flexible to adjust to these changes. The public library should also help to preserve the culture, history and traditions of the local community and make them readily available.

The public library, by organizing activities and exploiting its resources, should encourage artistic and cultural development in people of all ages. The library is also an important social centre for individuals and groups to meet both formally and informally. This is of special importance in communities where other meeting places are not available.

3.4.7   Information services

The rapid development of information technology has brought a vast amount of information within reach of all those with access to electronic media. Information provision has always been a key role of the public library and the ways in which information can be collected, accessed and presented have changed radically in recent years. The public library has a number of roles in providing information:

- providing access to information at all levels
- collecting information about the local community and making it readily accessible, often in co-operation with other organizations
- training people of all ages in the use of information and the associated technology
- guiding users to the appropriate information sources
- providing opportunities for disabled people to have independent access to information
- acting as a gateway to the information world by making it accessible to

all, thus helping to bridge the gap between 'the information rich' and 'the information poor'.

The dramatic development of the Internet has been largely unstructured and uncontrolled. The vast amount of information that can be accessed via the Internet is of variable quality and accuracy and a key role of the librarian is to guide users to accurate information sources, which will meet their requirements.

▶ In Horsens, Denmark, the public library has set up an Information Booth to supply individuals with governmental, regional and local information, and to give help in completing forms and directing people to the right public department. Consumer questions are also answered. Both printed material and the Internet are used in dealing with enquiries (**http://www.bibliotek.horsens.dk**).

▶ In Medellin, Colombia, Comfenalco Public Library has developed a website with up-to-date information about the city, including institutions, personalities, cultural events and procedures related to public services. It also publishes a series of guides on questions most frequently raised by users (**http://www.comfenalcoantioquia.com/sil**).

3.4.8 Services to community groups

The public library should be at the centre of the community if it is to play a full part in its activities. It should, therefore, work with other groups and organizations in the community. This will include departments of government and local government, the business community and voluntary organizations. An analysis of the information needs of these bodies should be conducted, and services be provided to meet these needs. This will not only help the organizations involved but will also demonstrate, in a practical way, the value of the public library to people in the community who are likely to have some influence on the future of the library service. Many public libraries, for example, provide an information service to local government politicians and staff, giving a practical demonstration of the value of the public library.

▶ Essex County Library, England, creates websites for voluntary organizations. It makes a small charge at below the commercial level.
▶ Grant funds were used in Arizona, USA, to provide a computer lab in the library for use by children and adults from the Hualapai tribe.
▶ In the West Midlands region of England, a project (INTER-ALL) has been developed supported by funding from the European regional Development Fund to provide information to small businesses. Learning and information centres are being established in 13 libraries in the region, supported by 15 full-time posts (**http://www.wm-libraries.org.uk**).

3.4.9 Services to special user groups

Potential users who, for whatever reason, are unable to use the regular services of the library have a right to equal access to library services. The library should, therefore, establish ways of making library material and services accessible to these users. These will include:

- special transport, e.g., mobile libraries, book-boats and other forms of transport to serve those living in isolated areas
- services taken to the home of those people who are housebound
- services taken to factories and industrial premises for employees
- services for those confined in institutions, e.g., prisons and hospitals
- special equipment and reading materials for those with physical and sensory disabilities, e.g., hearing impaired and visually impaired people
- special materials for people with learning difficulties, e.g., easy-to-read materials and cassettes
- services for immigrants and new citizens to help them to find their way within a different society and to provide access to media of their native culture
- electronic communication, e.g., Internet catalogues.

Services for people with special needs can be enhanced by the use of new technology, for example, speech synthesizers for the visually impaired, online access catalogues for those in isolated areas or unable to leave their home, connections to remote sites for distance learning. Mainstream service provision, for example, public access catalogues (OPACs) can often be adapted to meet the needs of those with physical and sensory disabilities. Those who can benefit the most from technological developments are often the least able to afford the investment needed. Innovative schemes should, therefore, be developed by the public library to exploit the new technology in order to make services available to as many people as possible.

Services for ethnic groups in the community and for indigenous peoples should be developed in consultation with the group concerned. They are likely to include:

- the employment of staff from the group in the library
- collections including the native literature of the group and reflecting the oral tradition and non-written knowledge of the people
- the application of special conditions, developed in conjunction with local people, to culturally sensitive material.

3.4.10 The library in the community

Library services can also be provided in a variety of places in the community where people congregate.

> Library services are provided at Metro stations in Santiago, Chile.
> Beach libraries are provided in Catalonia, Spain and in Portugal during the summer months.
> Many forms of transport are used to deliver library services. Book mobiles are common in many countries. There are book boats in Norway and Indonesia, where bicycles and pedicabs are also used, donkeys in Peru, which transport laptop computers as well as books, camels in Kenya and donkey-carts in Zimbabwe. Mopeds are used to deliver books to the home or office in Apeldoorn, Netherlands.
> In parts of South Africa library services are supplied to informal settlements or squatter areas with no infrastructure. This is done in a variety of ways, for example, from car boots, steel cabinets in clinics, cargo containers, under a tree or provided by individuals or shops to other members of the community. Block loans are provided to schools and old people's homes and storytelling and school project information

is available at after-care centres for children unable to go the library.

▸ In Colombia, steel cabinets containing about 300 books, a bench and a space for a billboard are provided in places where people congregate. They are open for about two hours a day.

▸ In Manassas, Virginia, USA, a mall store-front houses the state's first electronic library. It has no books but provides computing and technology courses and virtual library services. Services are free to county residents.

3.4.11 Reading promotion and literacy

Reading, writing and the ability to use numbers are basic prerequisites to being an integrated and active member of society. Reading and writing are also the basic techniques needed for making use of new communication systems. The public library should support activities that will enable people to make the best use of modern technology. It should support other institutions that are combating illiteracy and promoting media competence. It can achieve this by:

- promoting reading
- providing appropriate materials for those with poor literacy skills
- working with other agencies in the community involved in combating illiteracy
- participating in campaigns to combat illiteracy and improve numeracy
- organizing events to promote an interest in reading, literature and media culture
- promoting and providing training in the use of computer technology
- promoting awareness of new developments in the media market
- helping people to find the information they need in the appropriate format
- co-operating with teachers, parents and other contact persons to help new citizens acquire the necessary educational skills that will help them to manage their lives in the new context.

The public library provides a range of creative literature and can use promotional techniques to bring its variety and range to the attention of its users. It can also organize interactive programmes that enable users to exchange views about books that they have read.

‣ An interactive programme developed in Wandsworth, England, uses multimedia software to encourage readers to experiment with their reading and engage in dialogue about books they have read.
‣ Offaly and Limerick County Libraries, Ireland, in partnership with literacy students, tutors, local literacy organizers and the National Adult Literacy Agency, are active agents in literacy provision. They make a wide range of books and other materials available to adult literacy students and their tutors and generally promote a reading culture.
‣ In Singapore, the library works with a self-help group, training women who are learning English. Classes are held in the libraries, which support the programme by providing the resources needed.
‣ Comfenalco library in Medellin, Colombia, has a weekly page in the main city newspaper that includes reviews and comments on books for children.

3.5   Customer care

The policies and procedures of the library should be based on the needs and convenience of the users and not for the convenience of the organization and its staff. Quality services can only be delivered if the library is sensitive to the needs of its users and shapes its services to meet those needs. Satisfied users are the best advocates of the library service.

The public library should have a positive policy of customer care. This means ensuring that in all policy planning, design of libraries and of systems, preparation of operational procedures and drafting of information and publicity material, a positive effect on the user should be a prime objective. The following actions should be elements in a customer care policy:

• the image projected by all libraries must be neutral and objective
• staff should be courteous, friendly, respectful and helpful at all times

- there should be a regular programme of staff training in customer care
- all staff should receive basic awareness training on how to deal with people with disabilities or from ethnic minorities
- jargon should be avoided in all forms of communication, verbal and written
- staff should have a friendly and informative telephone manner
- methods of communication with the users must be provided, e.g., billboards, bulletins, website
- library services should be properly planned, adequately prepared and reliable
- the design of the library should be as convenient and inviting as possible
- opening hours should be convenient for the users
- open public access catalogues should be available on the Internet so that the user can access services from home and outside opening hours
- there should be efficient renewal and reservation services
- services should be delivered beyond the library building when users' needs require it
- users should receive a response in the shortest possible time; letters and other forms of communication should be answered promptly and courteously
- equipment should be provided to make library use convenient, e.g., drop-in boxes for returning materials out of hours, self-service issue and return equipment in the library, answering machines for communicating with the library out of hours
- all printed information about services should be available in appropriate alternative formats, e.g., large print, tape; they should also be available in minority languages
- when resources allow, good quality electronic equipment should be provided in the library including special equipment for the partially sighted and hearing impaired.

3.5.1   User participation

Customers should be involved in service development:

- by asking them through surveys what services they use and require

- by analysing and responding to users' complaints
- by monitoring users' reactions to services and new initiatives
- by ensuring the input received from users is considered in the development of policy and procedures
- by providing feedback to users about the effects of their input on service development
- by providing suggestion boxes and a complaints and commendations procedure.

3.6   User education

The public library should help its users develop skills that will enable them to make the most effective use of the library's resources and services. Library staff must act as information navigators to help users of all ages to make the most effective use of information and communications technology, and programmes of user education should be developed. As the new technologies become more commonly available, the role of the public library both in providing access to these technologies and in helping people learn how to make best use of them is of vital importance.

Guided tours of the library should take place regularly to introduce people to the library building and services and how to use its tools, for example, catalogues and technical equipment. These guided tours have to be carefully planned according to the needs of those taking part. Tours for groups should be organized in co-operation with the institution from which they come.

▶ Public libraries in Singapore provide orientation programmes for new and existing users. Tours of the library are organized for classes from schools and kindergartens. Information literacy programmes are provided at different levels to assist users in their search for information.

▶ The public library in Rijeka, Croatia, organized workshops and seminars to introduce the use of the Internet to targeted groups in the community. The courses were aimed at different groups each year (http://www.grad-rijeka.tel.hr).

▶ Ten libraries in New Jersey, USA, were given grants to create computer training centres. Grants supported the purchase of PCs and the presentation of computer training courses on a variety of topics.

3.7   Co-operation and resource sharing

Overall service to the community is enhanced when libraries develop links for exchanging information, ideas, services and expertise. Such co-operation results in less duplication of service, a combining of resources for maximum effect, and an overall improvement in community services. In addition, individual community members may in some cases be of great assistance in helping the library to carry out special tasks or projects.

3.7.1   Formal links

The library should establish formal links with other organizations in the local community, for example, schools, cultural institutions such as museums, galleries and archives, literacy programmes, chambers of commerce or boards of trade. The links should be used to co-ordinate the resources and efforts of each partner and thereby jointly improve services to the community.

3.7.2   Relations with schools

One of the most important institutional relationships for a public library is that with the local schools and the education system in the service area. Types of linkages and/or forms of co-operation include:

- sharing resources
- sharing staff training
- co-operative collection development
- co-operative programming
- co-ordination of electronic services and networks
- co-operation in the development of learning tools
- class visits to the public library
- joint reading and literacy promotion
- programme of web-awareness for children
- sharing of telecommunications and network infrastructures
- jointly arranged authors' visits.

(See *IFLA/UNESCO School Library Manifesto*.)

3.7.3 Resource sharing

Each library collection is in some degree unique. No collection can contain all the materials that the members of its public require. Libraries, therefore, can greatly enhance services to their users by providing them with access to the collections of other libraries. Libraries can participate in resource-sharing schemes at any level, local, regional, national and international, involving libraries of a wide range of organizations with information resources.

The library should also make its collection available for loan to other libraries through participation in a network, for example, in a union catalogue or in a local network of information providers, such as schools, colleges and universities.

3.7.4 Bibliographic records

The library should classify and catalogue its resources according to accepted international or national bibliographic standards. This facilitates their inclusion in wider networks.

3.7.5 Borrowing from other libraries

In order to meet the information needs of users the library should borrow materials from other libraries both within the same organization and beyond. The library should establish interlending policies, which address such issues as:

- lending materials to other public libraries
- the type of materials it is prepared to lend or not to lend
- the length of time for which materials will be lent
- when it will request materials from other libraries
- methods of shipment
- how the costs of the service will be met
- action to be taken if materials are lost or damaged.

3.8 Electronic networks

Public libraries are instruments of equal opportunity and must provide a safety-net against alienation and social exclusion from technological advance by becoming the electronic doorway to information in the digital age. They should enable all citizens to have access to the information that will enable them to manage their lives at the local level, to acquire essential information about the democratic process and to participate positively in an increasingly global society.

The library should provide access to the resources of the library and to those of other libraries and information services through the creation and maintenance of and participation in effective electronic networks at all levels from local to international. This can include participation in community networks, programmes to develop technologically advanced communities and electronic networks linking two or more agencies. They should also be part of national information policies.

▸ A virtual public library has been introduced in Denmark. It is possible to gain access to the catalogues of all public libraries plus the biggest research and special libraries. People are able to order an item from anywhere in the country and collect it at their local library (**http://www.bibliotek.dk**).

▸ In the UK, a number of libraries participate in the 'Ask-a Librarian' initiative. This is an electronic reference enquiry service online 24 hours a day, 365 days of the year. Enquiries are sent online and automatically re-routed to the rota library. The library then responds direct to the enquirer (**http://www.earl.org.uk/ask/**).

3.8.1 User access

The library should provide free public access to the Internet/world wide web to enable all citizens, regardless of economic means, to have access to information available in electronic form. It should have at least one public-access workstation with Internet access and a printer that is not shared with staff.

3.8.2 Remote access

The library should exploit information and communications technology to enable the public to gain access to as many of its electronic resources and services as possible from their home, school or workplace. If possible they should be made accessible 24 hours a day, seven days a week. Making the library catalogue available on the Internet increases its accessibility to the public, and to other libraries, and improves the quality of the service.

> ▶ DelAWARE, developed by Delaware State Library, USA, gives all Delaware citizens access to library information services and the Internet, regardless of geographic location or economic circumstances. It provides a variety of statewide online products and services, state government information, a subject guide to selected Internet sites and links to all types of Delaware libraries (**http://www.lib.de.us**).

3.8.3 Staff access

Library staff should have access to the Internet/world wide web to enable them to provide better reference and readers' advisory service to users. Staff should have regular training in using the Internet.

3.8.4 Information navigator

The public library's role is becoming one of mediator, of being the public's electronic doorway to digital information and of helping citizens cross the 'digital divide' to a better future. The librarian's role is increasingly one of 'information navigator' ensuring that the user gets accurate and reliable information.

> ▶ Regional and local libraries in Denmark are producing a Public Libraries Net-Guide, which provides valuable descriptions of a wide range of websites. The sites are evaluated by librarians. A similar guide for children and young adults is also being produced (**http://www. fng.dk**).

3.9 Access to services

Physical accessibility is one of the major keys to the successful delivery of public library services. Services of high quality are of no value to those who are unable to access them. Access to services should be structured in a way that maximizes convenience to users and potential users.

3.9.1 Location of service outlets

Public library service outlets should be located for the maximum convenience of residents of the community. If possible they should be near the centre of transport networks and close to areas of community activity, for example, shops, commercial centres, cultural centres. Where appropriate the public library may share buildings with other services such as arts centres, museums, art galleries, community centres and sports facilities. This can help to attract users and achieve capital and operational economies.

The outlet should be highly visible and easily reached by foot, public transport, where available, or by private vehicle. In well-developed urban and suburban areas a public library should be available within a journey by private vehicle of about 15 minutes.

> ▸ In Singapore, libraries are located in the town centres of government housing estates. Children's libraries are located on the ground floor of apartment blocks and are within five minutes' walk of most children in the neighbourhood.

3.9.2 Opening hours

In order to provide the best possible access to the library service, the library must be open at times of maximum convenience to those who live, work and study in the community.

3.10 Library buildings

In general when planning a library, the librarian and governing body should consider the following elements:

- the function of the library
- the size of the library
- designated spaces
- design features
- accessible shelving
- sign-posting
- the ambience of the library
- electronic and audiovisual equipment
- safety
- parking.

3.10.1 The function of the library

The library should have adequate space to implement the full range of library services that are consistent with the library's strategic plan and that meet local, area or national standards/guidelines.

3.10.2 The size of the library

The amount of floor-space required by a public library depends on such factors as the unique needs of the individual community, the functions of the library, the level of resources available, the size of the collection, the space available and the proximity of other libraries. Because these elements will vary significantly from country to country and between different building projects it is not possible to propose a universal standard on the space required for a public library. Local standards have been developed and examples from Ontario, Canada and Barcelona, Spain are included in an appendix and may be of use in the planning process (see Appendix 4 'Library Building Standards').

3.10.3 Designated spaces

The library should include space for services to adults, children and young adults and for family use. It should aim to provide a range of materials to meet the needs of all groups and individuals in the community (see Chapter 4 'Collection development').

The range of functions provided and the space available for each will depend on the size of the library. In planning a new library the following should be considered for inclusion:

- the library collection including, books, periodicals, special collections, sound recordings and video cassettes and other non-print and digital resources
- reader seating space for adults, children and young adults to use for leisure reading, serious study, group work and one–one tutoring; quiet rooms should be provided
- outreach services: space should be provided to house special collections and preparation areas for outreach services
- staff facilities, including work space (including desks or PC workstations), rest space for eating and relaxing during breaks and meeting rooms where staff can meet with colleagues and supervisors in private
- meeting room space for large and small community groups, which should have separate access to the washrooms and to the exterior to enable meetings to be held while the library is closed
- technology, including public access workstations, printers, CD-ROM stations, copiers, microfilm/fiche readers, public typewriters and facilities for listening to recorded sound
- special equipment, including atlas cases, newspaper racks, self-service book circulation, dictionaries, wall-mounted display racks, display stands, filing cabinets, map cases etc.
- sufficient space for ease of circulation by both public and staff; this can be 15%–20% of public areas and 20%–25% in staff areas
- in larger libraries a café area for the public is a desirable facility
- space must be allowed for the mechanical services of the library, e.g., elevators, heating, ventilation, maintenance, storage of cleaning materials, etc.

3.10.4 Design features

The library should guarantee easy access for all users and in particular persons with physical and sensory disabilities. The following features should be included in the planning of a new library:

- the exterior of the library should be well lit and identified with signs clearly visible from the street
- the entrance of the library should be clearly visible and located on that part of the building that most users approach.
- the library should focus on eliminating barriers to use
- there should be no design features that limit the ability of an individual or groups to use any part of the library
- care should be taken to avoid steps as much as possible in both interior and exterior design
- lighting levels should comply with those stated in international or national standards
- libraries that occupy two or more floors should provide elevators that are close to the library entrance and that easily accommodate wheelchairs and child strollers
- the library should provide facilities for the return of library materials when the library is closed; after-hours deposit boxes should be both theft and waterproof
- a library should undertake an 'accessibility' audit on a regular basis to confirm that there are no barriers to easy use
- local, national or international standards on making public buildings accessible to the disabled should be followed, wherever possible.

3.10.5   Accessible shelving

Materials should be displayed on open shelves and arranged at a height within easy reach for users. All shelving should be adjustable and preferably on lockable wheels so that it can easily be moved. The furniture in the children's section should be appropriately sized. Shelves should be of accessible height and width for persons using a wheelchair.

3.10.6   Sign-posting

The library's exterior signs not only identify the particular function of the building but are also the library's most basic form of publicity. Signs should therefore be carefully planned to communicate an appropriate image of the library. Internal areas of the library and parts of the collection should be clearly identified by signs of a professional standard so that users can easily find them, for example, the library catalogue, magazines, reference services, the children's area, washrooms, Internet stations, copy machines etc. Signs should also be posted in Braille where necessary. Where appropriate, signs should be provided in languages used by ethnic groups in the community. A sign displaying the opening hours of the library should be clearly visible from outside the library. Talking kiosks could also be considered to help all users find their way in the library. Directional signs should be erected in nearby streets and town centres to guide the public to the library.

3.10.7 The ambience of the library

The library should provide a physical setting for the library service that is inviting to the public and that provides:

- adequate space to store and display the library collection
- adequate, comfortable and attractive space for the public to make proper and convenient use of the library's services
- sufficient space for the library staff to carry out their duties in an efficient and comfortable setting
- adequate space and flexibility for the future.

The climate of the library should be maintained at a comfortable temperature, using efficient heating and air conditioning. Humidity control helps to protect the stock as well as increasing the comfort of the library.

Larger libraries may include a café open either throughout the opening hours of the library or for special occasions. Such facilities are sometimes contracted out to a commercial provider.

▶ In Singapore, the concept of 'lifestyle' libraries is being introduced. They include a café, music listening-posts and a virtual community for students. All libraries are open seven days a week.

3.10.8   Electronic and audiovisual equipment

As a major function of the public library is to bridge the gap between the information rich and the information poor, it has also to provide access to the necessary electronic, computer and audiovisual equipment. This will include personal computers with Internet access, public access catalogues, microform readers, tape recorders, slide projectors and equipment for the visually and physically handicapped. Wiring should be up-to-date and easily accessible for alterations at a later date. It should also be inspected regularly.

3.10.9   Safety

Every effort should be made to ensure that the library is safe for the public and the staff. Smoke and fire alarms should be provided and security protection for staff and resources. The location of fire extinguishers and emergency exits should be clearly marked. Staff should be trained in first aid and first aid supplies be made readily available. Evacuation drills should be carried out regularly. The library manager in co-operation with the emergency services should prepare a disaster plan to be put into action in the event of a serious incident, for example fire.

3.10.10 Parking

Where users travel to the library in private vehicles there should be sufficient safe and well lit parking either at or close to the library with appropriately identified spaces for persons with disabilities. If bicycles are a common mode of transport, secure cycle racks should be provided outside the library.

4

Collection development

'Specific services and materials must be provided for those users who cannot, for whatever reason, use the regular services and materials, for example linguistic minorities, people with disabilities or people in hospital or prison.

All age groups must find material relevant to their needs.

Collections and services have to include all types of appropriate media and modern technologies as well as traditional materials. High quality and relevance to local needs and conditions are fundamental. Material must reflect current trends and the evolution of society, as well as the memory of human endeavour and imagination.

Collections and services should not be subject to any form of ideological, political or religious censorship, nor commercial pressures.'

(IFLA/UNESCO Public Library Manifesto, 1994)

4.1   Introduction

The public library should provide equality of access to a range of resources that meets the needs of its users for education, information, leisure and personal development. The library should provide access to the heritage of its society and develop diverse cultural resources and experiences. Constant interaction and consultation with the local community will help to ensure this objective is achieved.

4.2 Collection management policy

Each public library system requires a written collection management policy, endorsed by the governing body of the library service. The aim of the policy should be to ensure a consistent approach to the maintenance and development of the library collections and access to resources.

It is imperative that collections continue to be developed on an ongoing basis to ensure that people have a constant choice of new materials and to meet the demands of new services and of changing levels of use. In the light of today's technological advances, the policy must reflect not only a library's own collections but also strategies for accessing information available throughout the world.

The policy should be based upon library standards developed by professional staff related to the needs and interests of local people, and reflecting the diversity of society. The policy should define the purpose, scope and content of the collection, as well as access to external resources.

▸ In some libraries in the Russian Federation a council of readers helps to determine the acquisition policy.

4.2.1 Content of the policy

The policy may proceed from statements of universal applicability that are relevant to all library services, through more general statements that are relevant to particular countries, or regions, to statements that are specific to particular library services and could include the following elements.

Universal

- Article XIX of the Declaration of Human Rights
- IFLA statement on freedom of access to information
- statements on intellectual freedom, free access to library collections
- freedom of information
- consideration of the International Copyright Convention
- *IFLA/UNESCO Public Library Manifesto.*

General

- purpose of the collection management policy and its relation to the corporate plan of the library service
- long and short term objectives
- access strategies
- history of the collection and/or library service
- identification of relevant legislation.

Specific

- analysis of community needs
- priorities of the library service
- parameters of the collection, including special collections and collections for special needs, such as multicultural material, literacy and resources for people with disabilities
- selection and discard principles and methods
- budget allocation
- responsibility within the organization for collection development, selection and discard
- access to electronic resources including online access to periodicals, databases and other information sources
- the role of the library as an electronic gateway to information
- co-operative relationships with other libraries and organizations
- preservation and conservation policies
- auditing requirements: accessioning, recording, control, discard, sale or disposal
- financial accountability
- donations policy
- complaints procedure
- a resource management plan assessing the current and future needs of the collections
- review and assessment of the policy.

This is not an exhaustive list but an indication of some of the issues that may be included.

4.3   Range of resources

The public library should provide a wide range of materials in a variety of formats and in sufficient quantity to meet the needs and interests of the community. The culture of the local community and society must be reflected in the resource collection. Public libraries must keep abreast of new formats and new methods of accessing information. All information should be as readily available as possible, irrespective of format. The development of local information sources and resources is vital.

4.3.1   Collections

The following categories of library materials may be represented in a typical public library, although this list is not exhaustive:

- fiction and non-fiction for adults, young adults and children
- reference works
- access to databases
- periodicals
- local, regional and national newspapers
- community information
- government information, including information by and about local administrations
- business information
- local history resources
- genealogical resources
- resources in the primary language of the community
- resources in minority languages in the community
- resources in other languages
- music scores
- computer games
- toys
- games and puzzles
- study materials.

4.3.2   Formats

The following formats may be included in a public library collection although this list is not exhaustive and new formats are continually appearing:

- books, both hard and soft covers
- pamphlets and ephemera
- newspapers and periodicals including cuttings files
- digital information through the Internet
- online databases
- CD-ROM databases
- software programmes
- microforms
- tapes and compact discs (CDs)
- digital versatile discs (DVDs)
- videocassettes
- laser discs
- large print materials
- braille materials
- audio books
- electronic books
- posters.

4.4   Collection development

Collections complement services and should not be seen as an end in themselves, unless their specified primary purpose is the preservation and conservation of resources for future generations.

Large collections are not synonymous with good collections, particularly in the new digital world. The relevance of the collection to the needs of the local community is more important than the size of the collection.

Collection size is determined by many factors, including space, financial resources, catchment population of the library, proximity to other libraries, regional role of the collections, access to electronic resources, assessment of local needs, acquisition and discard rates, and policy of stock exchanges with other libraries.

4.4.1   Criteria for collections

The main criteria for collections should be:

- a range of resources that cater for all members of the community
- resources in formats that enable all members of the community to make use of the library service
- inflow of new titles
- inflow of new books
- a wide range of fiction categories and of non-fiction subject coverage
- provision of non-print resources
- access to external resources such as libraries of other institutions, electronic databases, local societies, government departments or the community's knowledge of oral cultures
- discard of old, worn and outdated books, non-print resources and information sources.

4.5   Collection maintenance principles

Public libraries of any size will contain materials in a variety of formats. Collection maintenance applies equally to all materials whatever their format. Materials on open access should be in good physical condition and contain current information. A smaller, high quality stock will result in more usage than a large stock with a high proportion of old, worn and outdated books, in which newer titles can be lost among mediocre stock. Using outdated reference material can result in the user being given inaccurate information.

Materials in electronic formats complement book collections and will replace them in certain areas. Reference works and periodicals on the Internet and on CDs are viable alternatives to printed formats.

4.5.1   Acquisition and discards

The library collection is a dynamic resource. It requires a constant inflow of new material and outflow of old material to ensure that it remains relevant to the community and at an acceptable level of accuracy.

Acquisition rates are more significant than collection size. The acquisition rate is often determined largely by the size of the resource budget. However, it can also be affected by other factors, for example:

- the number of books published in local languages
- the population served
- the level of use
- the multicultural and linguistic diversity
- age distribution of the population
- special needs such as people with disabilities or older persons
- access to online information.

The size and quality of the stock should reflect the needs of the community.

4.5.2 Reserve stocks

It may be necessary to maintain a collection of older and lesser-used books on shelves not directly accessible to the public. This should only contain books that have a current or future use and that cannot be replaced or found in any other format. This may include special subject collections that are used on a regular, if limited, basis and out-of-print fiction. Books that contain outdated information or are in poor condition and can be replaced, should be discarded and not held in a reserve stock. It is efficient to maintain a co-operative reserve with other libraries. The maintenance of a reserve stock should be a regular and on-going activity. The availability of a wide range of information on the Internet and electronic databases reduces the need for public libraries to keep extensive reserve stocks.

4.5.3 Interlending

No library or library service can be self-sufficient in stock, and an efficient and effective interlibrary loan system should be an essential part of every public library service. Within a library service with several outlets a regular programme of exchange of stock between libraries makes maximum use of the stock and provides users with a greater variety of titles from which to choose.

4.6 Standards for book collections

The following proposed standards relate to book collections. Local and financial circumstances could lead to variations in these proposed standards. Where resources are severely limited these may be regarded as target figures and medium and long-term strategies should be developed to work towards achieving these standards in the future.

> ‣ As a general guide an established book collection should be between 1.5 to 2.5 books per capita
> ‣ The minimum stock level for the smallest service point should not be less than 2500 books.

In the smallest collections materials for children, adult fiction and adult non-fiction may be provided in equal proportions. In larger collections the percentage of non-fiction titles will tend to increase. These ratios can vary according to the needs of the local community and the role of the public library. Relevant collections to serve the needs of young adults should be developed (see *IFLA guidelines for library services to young adults*). Where the library has a strong educational role this is likely to be reflected in the composition of the stock.

Where reliable population figures are not available alternative methods of developing standards are needed. The estimated size of the community served, the size of the library, and the number of current and anticipated users can be used as a basis for developing standards for the size of the collection. Comparisons with a number of existing libraries serving communities of a similar size and make-up can be used to determine a target figure for the size of the collection and the resources needed to maintain it.

4.7 Standards for electronic information facilities

The development of standards for the provision of electronic information facilities is at an early stage. Current standards include the following:

> A standard of one computer access point per 5000 population has been used in Canada.

> A recently developed standard in England recommends that the total number of workstations, including those for online catalogues, that are available for public use, should not be less than 6 per 10 000 population.

> In Queensland, Australia it is recommended that the following be provided:
>   • for populations up to 50 000 – one PC per 5000 population.
>   • for populations over 50 000 – one PC per 5000 population for 50 000 population and one PC per each additional 10 000 population.
>
> These standards recommend that at least half the public PCs should have access to the Internet and all should have access to a printer.

4.8 Collection development programme for new libraries

An assessment is required of the demographics of the community in the catchment areas of proposed new library developments to determine the initial mix of collections. The development of local and regional standards should be undertaken to take account of variations in the catchment population to be served by the new library. The following recommended standards relate to book provision. Additional standards will be required for other media.

4.8.1 Establishment phase

A basic collection should be established in new libraries to serve the needs of the general population within the catchment area. A sufficient range and depth of resources to meet general needs should be the aim at this stage rather than comprehensive coverage. The interlibrary loan system should be at its peak utilization during this phase to supplement the developing collections. In some countries materials from a national or provincial centre are used to supplement the local stock.

> ▶ Ideally a new library should be established with a minimum base stock of 1.0 book per capita.

Where this is not achievable a modest growth plan should be implemented to establish this minimum base stock over a period of three years. Access to electronic information sources should also be included in this phase of development.

4.8.2   Consolidation phase

The objective under this phase is to achieve growth in the stock size, range and depth. Special conditions of the population are taken into account and collections developed to meet the more in-depth needs of the population served. The book discard factor comes into play and the collection growth rate decreases as discards begin to offset acquisitions.

> ▶ A growth to 2.0 books per capita would be a modest target over a three-year period.

4.8.3   Steady-state phase

The collections meet the needs of the community in depth, range and quantity. The quality of collections is maintained by acquisition rates matching discard rates. New formats are accommodated within the collections as they become available and access is provided to the widest possible range of resources through the use of technology.

4.8.4   Content creation

The service should become a content creator and a preserver of local community resources. Content creation includes publication of information booklets and the development of web content by providing access to information about the library or held by the library in printed formats. This positions the library as an electronic gateway by the creation of links to useful web pages.

▶ Eight public libraries in Vejle, Denmark, co-operate in creating a website covering all the cultural events in the region. It also records details of more than 2000 local organizations and supplies them with a web presentation to promote their activities (**http://www.netopnu.dk**).

4.9   Acquisition and discard rates

For general book stock in an established library service the following acquisition rates may be applied:

Population	Books per capita per annum	Books per 1000 population per annum
Below 25 000	0.25	250
25 000–50 000	0.225	225
50 000+	0.20	200

The following examples suggest the size of book stock for communities of different sizes.

Scenario 1

- Established library service serving 100 000 population
- Median book stock of 200 000 volumes
- Annual acquisition rate of 20 000 volumes

Scenario 2

- Established library service serving 50 000 population
- Median book stock of 100 000 volumes
- Annual acquisition rate of 11 250 volumes

Scenario 3

- Established library service serving 20 000 population
- Median book stock of 40 000 volumes
- Annual acquisition rate of 5000 volumes.

4.9.1 Small libraries and mobile libraries

The general acquisition rates would be inadequate to meet the needs of small libraries and mobile libraries where stock numbers are limited. All libraries require a certain minimum stock in order to provide a sufficient range of books from which users may make their selection. The acquisition rate of 250 books per 1000 population may not be relevant in the smallest service points, where physical limitations may reduce stock levels below the minimum recommended level of 2500 volumes. In these cases the acquisition rates, renewal rates or exchange rates should be based upon the collection size rather than the population served, and be in the order of 100% or more per annum. An efficient interlibrary loan system is essential in these situations.

4.9.2 Special collections

General acquisition and discard rates may not be relevant to some parts of the collection or to particular special collections or where special circumstances prevail. In these cases the collection policy must reflect the special needs. Particular examples of these exceptions are:

- indigenous resources – the public library has a role in maintaining and promoting collections of resources related to the culture of indigenous people and ensuring access to them
- local history resources – material relating to the history of the locality should be actively collected, preserved and made available
- libraries in communities with a high proportion of particular groups, e.g., children, retired people, young adults, indigenous peoples, ethnic minorities or unemployed people should reflect the needs of these groups in their collections and services
- reference collections – older reference material may need to be retained to provide historical data for research.

5

Human resources

'The public library has to be organised effectively and professional standards of operation must be maintained.

The librarian is an active intermediary between users and resources. Professional and continuing education of the librarian is indispensable to ensure adequate services.'

(IFLA/UNESCO Public Library Manifesto, 1994)

5.1   Introduction

Staff are a vitally important resource in the operation of a library. Staff expenses normally represent a high proportion of a library's budget. In order to provide the best possible service to the community it is necessary to maintain well trained and highly motivated staff to make effective use of the resources of the library and to meet the demands of the community. Staff should be available in sufficient numbers to carry out these responsibilities.

The management of library staff is itself an important task. All staff should have a clear understanding of the policy of the library service, well-defined duties and responsibilities, properly regulated conditions of employment and salaries that are competitive with other similar jobs.

5.2   The skills of library staff

The public library is a service aimed at all members of the community who will have varied and changing needs. Public library staff will require a range of skills and qualities, including interpersonal skills, social awareness, teamwork and leadership and competence in the practices and procedures of the organization. The fundamental qualities and skills required of public library staff can be defined as:

- the ability to communicate positively with people
- the ability to understand the needs of users
- the ability to co-operate with individuals and groups in the community
- knowledge and understanding of cultural diversity
- knowledge of the material that forms the library's collection and how to access it
- an understanding of and sympathy with the principles of public service
- the ability to work with others in providing an effective library service
- organizational skills, with the flexibility to identify and implement changes
- imagination, vision and openness to new ideas and practice
- readiness to change methods of working to meet new situations
- knowledge of information and communications technology.

5.3   Staff categories

The following categories of staff are found in public libraries:

- qualified librarians
- library assistants
- specialist staff
- support staff.

In some countries there is an additional category of library technician, or para-professional, with an intermediate level of qualifications.

Staff in all categories may be appointed on either a full-time or part-time basis. In some countries two or more people share a single post, a practice known as job-sharing. This provides the opportunity to appoint and retain experienced staff who may not be able to work full-time.

5.3.1   Qualified librarians

Qualified librarians are professional staff who have undertaken a course of study in librarianship and information studies to degree or post-graduate level. A librarian designs, plans, organizes, implements, manages and evaluates library and information services and systems to meet the needs of the users of library and information services in the community. This will include collection development, the organization and exploitation of resources, the provision of advice and assistance to users in finding and using information and the development of systems that will facilitate access to the library's resources. Qualified librarians will have regular contact with members of the community that they serve. In order to fulfil its functions staff with expertise in specific areas, for example, children's librarians, information officers and reference librarians should form part of the professional team.

The following is a list of some of the duties of the qualified librarian. This list is not exhaustive nor is it likely that the qualified librarian will undertake all these activities simultaneously:

- analysing the resource and information needs of the community
- formulating and implementing policies for service development
- planning services to the public and participating in their delivery
- retrieving and presenting information
- answering reference and information enquiries using appropriate material
- assisting users in the use of library resources and information
- developing services to meet the needs of special groups, e.g., children
- creating and maintaining databases to meet the needs of the library and its users
- designing library and information services and systems to meet the needs of the public
- developing acquisition policies and systems for library resources
- managing and administering library and information systems
- cataloguing and classification of library materials
- promoting library services
- evaluating library services and systems and measuring their performance
- selecting, evaluating, managing and training staff
- budgeting
- strategic planning
- participation in planning the design and layout of new and refurbished libraries and of mobile libraries

- keeping up-to-date with current developments in librarianship and information services including the relevant technologies.

5.3.2 Library assistants

The duties of the library assistant include routine circulation functions and operational library tasks such as shelving, shelf-checking, processing library materials, data entry, filing, secretarial support and basic level reader enquiry work. Library assistants are the staff the public will come into contact with most frequently. It is essential, therefore, that they should have a high level of interpersonal and communication skills and receive appropriate training.

5.3.3 Specialist staff

Large public library services may employ specialist staff to carry out specific functions, for example, computer system managers, administrative, financial, training and marketing staff. Specialist staff may have a qualification in their specialism rather than in librarianship.

5.3.4 Support staff

Support staff include caretakers, cleaners, drivers and security staff. They carry out important functions, which contribute to the smooth operation of the library service. They should be regarded as an integral part of the library's staff.

5.3.5 The composition of the staff

The composition of the staff should, as far as possible, reflect the make-up of the population it serves. Where, for example, there is a significant number of people from a particular ethnic group within the community, the library staff should include members of that group. This demonstrates that the library is a service for all members of the local community and will help to attract users from all sections of the public.

5.4   Ethical standards

Public library staff have a responsibility to maintain high ethical standards in their dealings with the public, other members of staff and external organizations. All members of the public should be dealt with on an equal basis and every effort must be made to ensure that information provided is as full and accurate as possible. Librarians must not allow their personal attitudes and opinions to determine which members of the public are served and what materials are selected and displayed. The public must have confidence in the impartiality of the library staff if the library is to meet the needs of all members of the community. Library associations in some countries have developed codes of ethics, which can be used as models to introduce similar codes elsewhere. The IFLA/FAIFE website includes details of over 20 codes of ethics for librarians from various countries (**http://www.faife.dk/ ethics/codes.htm**).

5.5   The duties of library staff

The operation of a library should be a team effort with a close working relationship between all members of staff. It is important, however, that staff are used primarily for tasks related to their skills and qualifications. It is a wasteful use of scarce resources, for example, for qualified librarians to regularly carry out routine circulation functions. For the same reason it is not necessary to have a qualified librarian in every library regardless of size or circulation rate. Small libraries open for limited hours do not require the continuous presence of a qualified librarian. They should however be under the supervision of a member of the qualified staff. All users should have the opportunity of access to a qualified librarian. Staff should have a written contract at the time of their appointment, which clearly states their duties and responsibilities. These should not be changed without consulting the member of staff involved.

5.6   Staffing levels

The number of staff required in each library service will be affected by a range of factors, for example, the number of library buildings, their size and layout, the number of departments within each building, the level of use, services provided beyond the library and requirements for specialist staff. Where some services are provided or supplemented by a regional or national central agency this will have an impact on the number of staff required at local level. The level of available resources is also a critical factor. Allowing for these and other local differences the following basic staffing level (excluding support staff) is recommended:

> ▸ One full-time equivalent member of staff for 2500 population
> ▸ One-third of staff (excluding support staff) should be qualified librarians.

These are basic recommended levels, which will be affected by local circumstances. Where reliable population figures are not available staffing levels can be related to the size of the library, the range of its functions and the number of users. Another method of developing an appropriate staffing level for a library service is to carry out bench-marking with libraries of comparative size and similar characteristics.

5.7   Education of librarians

Qualified librarians will have undertaken a degree or post-graduate course in librarianship and information studies at a school of librarianship. To ensure that they remain in touch with the latest developments, librarians should maintain a process of continuing professional development on a formal and informal basis. It is important that public librarians maintain close links with the schools of librarianship in their country and are fully aware of course content. Whenever possible they should participate in the work of the schools, for example, by contributing lectures, assisting in interviewing of prospective students and other appropriate forms of co-operation.

5.8   Training

Training is a vital element of the activities of a public library. There must be a planned and continuous programme of training for staff at all levels, which should include both full-time and part-time staff. The rapid developments in information technology make the need for regular training even more essential, and the importance of networking and access to other information sources should be included in training programmes. Specialist and support staff should receive induction training in the functions and purpose of the public library and the context in which it operates.

In budgeting for the implementation of new systems, an element should be included for training. In large library services a post of training officer should be created to plan and implement the training programme. To ensure funds are available for training a set percentage of the budget should be earmarked for this function.

> It is recommended that 0.5%–1% of the total library budget should be earmarked for training purposes.

This level of funding for training should be maintained at times of budget reductions as the need for a well-trained staff is very important in such circumstances.

5.8.1 Mentoring

An effective and economical method of training is to introduce a system of mentoring. New staff work with a more experienced colleague who provides guidance and training. The mentor should be able to advise the new member of staff about issues relating to their work and employment. A checklist of the training provided by the mentor should be maintained to ensure that it is carried out effectively.

5.8.2 Contacts

In addition to in-service training staff should be given opportunities to attend short courses and conferences relevant to their ability to carry out their work. They should be encouraged to be active members of the relevant library association, as this creates links with other library staff and provides opportunities for an exchange of ideas and experience. It may also be possible to arrange staff exchanges with staff in other libraries, either in the same country or in a similar library in another country, which can be a valuable experience for all those involved.

5.9   Career development

In order to motivate and retain skilled staff opportunities for career development should be available at all levels. A scheme of performance appraisal should be in place that provides staff with an evaluation of current performance and guidance in improving and developing their skills. It also presents an opportunity to review career progression.

5.10   Working conditions

All library staff should have satisfactory working conditions and the conditions of employment should be clearly stated in the contract given to the new member of staff when they are employed. Salaries should be at a level appropriate to the level of work being undertaken and competitive with other similar jobs in the community.

5.10.1   Health and safety

The health and safety of staff must be a high priority and policies and procedures put in place to reduce risks. Consideration should be given to:

- good working conditions for staff
- ergonomically designed furniture and equipment
- availability of technical aids for employees with special needs and disabilities
- the drawing up of evacuation plans and their testing on a regular basis
- identified health and safety risks being rectified at the earliest opportunity
- ensuring that all equipment and cabling conforms with recognized safety standards
- the establishment of a staff health and safety committee
- appointment and training of staff as first-aid officers and fire wardens
- provision of safety devices for staff, particularly when staff work at nights or away from the library
- providing advanced driver training for staff who drive library vehicles

- protective clothing when required
- limiting the weight of cartons and loads on book trolleys.

Public libraries are often open for long hours including evenings and weekends. In creating work schedules for staff every effort should be made to ensure that their working hours provide them with adequate time off at appropriate times for social activity. It is vital that good labour relations are maintained and fostered with staff.

5.10.2 Anti-social behaviour

In any building freely accessible to the public, staff will occasionally encounter users who behave in an unpleasant and anti-social manner. Staff should be trained in how to deal with such situations and have alarm systems that can alert other staff. Senior staff should be immediately available to assist staff and full records of such occurrences should be kept. A support system involving other staff and people from other agencies, for example, social workers, should be developed to help library staff deal with these situations.

5.11 Volunteers

Where a library uses volunteer help from individuals in the community to assist library staff, a written policy should be in place defining the tasks of these volunteers and their relationship to the library operation and staff. Volunteers should not be used as a substitute for paid staff.

6

The management and marketing of public libraries

'A clear policy must be formulated defining objectives, priorities and services in relation to the local community needs. The public library has to be organised effectively and professional standards of operation must be maintained.'

(IFLA/UNESCO Public Library Manifesto, 1994)

6.1   Introduction

A successful public library is a dynamic organization working with other institutions and with individuals to provide a range of library and information services to meet the varied and changing needs of the community. To be effective it requires experienced, flexible and well trained managers and staff able to use a range of management techniques. This chapter deals with the key elements of public library management.

6.2   Management skills

Management of a public library involves a number of different skills:

- leadership and motivation
- maintaining effective relationships with governing and funding bodies
- planning and policy development
- building and maintaining networks with other organizations
- budget negotiations and management
- management of library resources
- staff management

- planning and development of library systems
- the management of change
- marketing and promotion
- community liaison and lobbying.

6.2.1 Leadership and motivation

The library manager has a vital role in advocating the value of public libraries as an integral part of an international, national and local infrastructure. He/she must promote public libraries to politicians and key stakeholders at all levels in order to ensure they are aware of the importance of public libraries and to attract adequate funding for their maintenance and development. The library manager must ensure that governing authorities are informed of new developments that may impact on public library services and are made aware that the library service is a key player in providing access to the delivery of new services.

The library manager is responsible for the motivation of staff and bringing energy, vitality and strength into the library service and its staff. The manager also plays a key role in managing the development of physical facilities and ensuring that the most effective use is made of resources, including information technology, to enable the library service to meet the library and information needs of the community.

6.2.2 Relationships with governing and funding bodies

To achieve its goals the public library needs adequate and sustained funding. It is very important that the library manager establishes and maintains a close and positive relationship with the bodies that govern the library service and provide its funding. The library manager as head of the public library service should have direct access to and involvement with the board or committee that is directly responsible for the library service. As well as formal meetings there should be regular informal contacts between the library manager and members of the governing body, and they should be kept well informed about the library service and current and future developments.

6.2.3   Planning and policy development

Planning ensures that:

- the library responds to the needs of the community
- the governing body, management and staff understand what the library is trying to achieve
- community funds are spent in an effective and responsible manner
- continuity of service is maintained regardless of changes of personnel
- the library expands the expectations of the community as new services are developed
- the library is able to respond effectively to change.

The determination of public library goals, short and long term objectives, strategies and performance measurement is necessary to ensure equitable, effective and efficient library service provision with access for all sectors of the community. Strategic and operational plans require formulation, documentation and adoption.

Planning should not take place in isolation but in conjunction with the governing and funding bodies, the library staff and the actual and potential clients served. A strategic plan must be user-focused and should include the following elements:

- review of achievements
- examination of needs
- identification of priorities and short term goals
- development of strategies for achieving goals
- identification of critical success factors
- budget allocation
- deployment of resources to achieve optimum performance
- measurement and evaluation of input and output performance
- reassessment of needs and policies.

6.2.4   Operational planning

An operational plan is necessary to ensure that the activities of the library service are focused on achieving the priorities and goals identified in the strategic plan. The plan should reflect the following elements:

- a focus on service to users
- the implementation of the priorities and goals of the strategic plan
- the formation of operational elements of the agreed strategies
- the development of clearly identified goals with manageable and achievable time frames
- the definition of achievable outputs for the level of inputs
- the participation of library staff who carry out the activities
- the allocation of responsibility to identified staff members for achieving outputs
- a programme for monitoring, evaluating and amending the plan at regular intervals.

By-laws or local legislation, specific policies and procedures may be needed and should be properly formulated, documented and communicated to all those involved. Business and marketing plans, market research, community needs analyses and surveys of users and non-users should form part of the management process.

Planning for the future should advocate positive change and flexibility and aim to minimize the impact of transition on services, staff and users. To achieve effective change, all stakeholders must be involved in the change process.

6.3   Building and maintaining networks

The library manager must ensure that networks are developed and maintained at national, regional and local level, using information and communications technology wherever appropriate. This enables a very wide range of resources to be brought to the user at a local level. The library manager should also develop good working relationships with other agencies in the community, for example, schools, other local government departments and voluntary organizations for the benefit of the users, and to confirm the public library's role at the centre of community activity. The library manager should, wherever possible, ensure that the library takes an active and positive role within the corporate structure of the parent organization.

6.4   Financial management

Financial management and financial planning are vitally important to ensure that the library operates efficiently (at optimum performance), economically (at minimum cost), and effectively (at maximum benefit). In order to achieve these aims the library manager should:

- look for ways of improving levels of funding from national, state or local government or from other sources
- prepare 3–5 year business plans based on the library's long term plans, including bids for the required funds
- allocate funds to support activities identified in the library's policy statement and based on the priorities previously determined
- establish partnerships, where appropriate, for co-operative purchasing to maximize the use of available funds
- undertake activity-based costing to determine the cost of activities and programmes and to facilitate future planning
- maintain a policy for the sustainable renewal of plant and equipment
- evaluate and implement automated techniques, wherever appropriate, to improve efficiency and effectiveness
- introduce systems that will ensure that all staff with responsibility for any part of the budget will be fully accountable for the expenditure of funds for which they are responsible
- improve staff productivity and efficiency.

6.5   Management of library resources

A major element of a library's budget is expenditure on library materials. The library manager should ensure that these funds are spent properly and in accordance with the agreed priorities of the library and that the materials are maintained and made available so that they can be of maximum benefit to the library user.

6.6   Staff management

Library staff are a vital element of the library's resources and staff salaries are normally the largest part of the library budget. It is very important that the management of staff should be sensitive, consistent and based on sound principles if staff are to work most effectively and with high levels of motivation and job satisfaction. The following are important elements of staff management:

- An equitable procedure for staff appointments. Job and person specifications should be drawn up prior to a post being advertised. Interviews should be conducted in a way that is fair to all applicants. Appointments should be based solely on professional judgment and suitability for the post and not be prejudiced by any other factors.
- Good communication between staff at all levels. Managers should review internal communication systems regularly to make sure staff are well informed about the policies and procedures of the library service.
- The opportunity for staff to participate in the development of policy and operational procedures. Initiative should be encouraged to make the best use of the skills and experience of staff. By bringing staff into the decision-making process they will feel they 'own' the policies and procedures of the service.
- The principles of affirmative action, including the creation of nominated positions for special needs areas, may be adopted.

6.7   Planning and development of library systems

To make the most effective use of resources the public library will require a variety of systems, for example circulation control, financial management, internal communications. The library manager should ensure that appropriate systems are introduced, making use of specialist staff for their development where necessary. Staff must be given adequate training in the use of such systems, the effectiveness of which must be reviewed regularly.

6.8   The management of change

In common with many other organizations public libraries are going through a period of unprecedented and ongoing change as a result of the rapid development of information technology and social and demographic change. This presents tremendous opportunities for the public library, as information provision is one of its primary roles. It also presents challenges to managers and staff to ensure that change can be introduced with the maximum effectiveness and the least stress on staff and the organization. Library managers must be aware of the issues arising from continuous and fundamental change and establish methods of dealing with them.

6.8.1   Planning for the future

Library managers should be aware of developments both within and outside librarianship that are likely to have an impact on service development. They should make time to read and study so that they can anticipate the effect of changes, particularly technological, on the future shape of the service. They should also ensure that policy-makers and other staff are kept informed of future developments.

6.9   Delegation

The library manager in charge of the public library service has ultimate responsibility for the service, in conjunction with the governing body. However, all library staff with responsibility for any resources of the library, whether materials, staff or library premises, have a managerial role, and this should be recognized by the library manager and the member of staff concerned. They should be given appropriate managerial training and participate in the policy development of the library whenever possible. Managerial responsibility should be delegated to staff at an appropriate lower level. It should be made clear what responsibilities are being delegated and what the reporting mechanism to senior managers is. Staff must be given training to enable them to carry out the delegated responsibilities effectively. A planned system of delegation makes best use of the skills and experience of a wide range of staff and provides opportunities for professional development. It also increases the number of people fully involved in the development and operation of the library service, improves job satisfaction and prepares staff for promotion when opportunities arise.

6.10   Management tools

A wide range of management tools can be used in a public library. Their relevance will depend on a number of factors, for example, the cultural context, the size and character of the service, the management style of other departments in the same organization and available experience and funding. The following are however important tools for public libraries in almost any situation:

- community needs analysis
- monitoring and evaluation
- performance measurement.

6.10.1 Community needs analysis

In order to provide services that meet the needs of the whole community, the public library has to establish the extent of those needs. As needs and expectations will change, this process will need to be repeated at regular intervals, perhaps every five years. A community needs assessment is a process in which the library collects detailed information about the local community and its library and information needs. Planning and policy development are based on the results of this assessment and in this way a match between services and needs can be achieved. In some countries the preparation of a community needs assessment is a legislative requirement of the local authority. The information to be collected will include:

- socio-demographic information about the local community e.g., the age and gender profile, ethnic diversity, educational level
- data about organizations in the community, e.g., educational institutions, health centres, hospitals, penal establishments, voluntary organizations
- information about business and commerce in the locality
- the catchment area of the library i.e. where library users live in relation to the library

- transport patterns in the community
- information services provided by other agencies in the community.

This is not an exhaustive list and further research would be required to establish what information is needed to form a community needs assessment in each situation. However, the principle of preparing a community profile, which will enable the librarian and the governing body to plan service development and promotion on the needs of the community, is an important one whatever the local context. The assessment should be complemented by regular customer surveys to establish what library and information services the public wants, at what level, and how they judge the services they receive. Survey work is a specialist skill and, where resources are available, a more objective result will be gained if the survey is carried out by an external organization.

6.10.2 Monitoring and evaluation

As the library service moves towards its goals, management must be accountable in terms of financial control and the monitoring and evaluation of library activities. Management must continually monitor the performance of the library service to ensure that strategies and operational results are achieving the set objectives. Statistics should be collected over time to allow trends to be identified. Community needs and satisfaction surveys, and performance indicators are valuable tools in monitoring the achievements of the library. Techniques should be developed to measure the quality of the services provided and their impact on the community. All programmes and services should be evaluated on a regular basis to ascertain whether they are:

- achieving the objectives and declared goals of the library
- actually and regularly provided
- meeting the needs of the community
- able to meet changing needs
- in need of improvement, new direction or redefinition
- adequately resourced
- cost effective.

Procedures and processes operating within the library also require constant evaluation and revision to increase efficiency and effectiveness.

6.10.3 Performance indicators

The availability of reliable performance information is a necessary tool for evaluation and the improvement of efficiency, effectiveness and quality of service. The collection of statistics related to resources, staff, services, circulation, activities etc. will provide data for planning, show accountability and assist informed management decision-making.

The following key performance indicators may be used to evaluate and monitor the achievement of the library's objectives.

Usage indicators

- loans per capita
- total library visits per capita
- membership as a percentage of the population
- loans per item i.e. turnover resources
- reference enquiries per capita
- loans per opening hour
- number of accesses to electronic services and other non-print materials.

Resource indicators

- total stock per capita
- provision of terminals/personal computers per capita
- provision of online public access computers (OPACs) per capita.

Human resource indicators

- ratio of full time equivalent (FTE) staff to population
- ratio of professional staff to population
- ratio of full time equivalent (FTE) staff to library use.

Qualitative indicators

- user satisfaction surveys
- enquiries satisfied.

Cost indicators

- unit costs for functions, services and activities
- staff costs per functions, e.g., books processed, programmes
- total costs per capita, per member, per visitor, per service point etc.

Comparative indicators

- bench-mark statistical data against other relevant and comparable library services, internationally, nationally and locally.

In addition to the collection and analysis of input and output service statistics, the unstated needs of non-users should be established by carrying out market research including the use of focus groups and community surveys.

Where reliable population statistics are not available it becomes more difficult to develop reliable performance indicators. Use can be made of estimated population totals, the comparison of costs with user and visitor statistics and bench-marking with other libraries with similar characteristics.

6.10.4 Performance measurement

Performance measurement has been used in public libraries for some years. Measurements or performance indicators are established to measure the input to libraries, that is the resources devoted to the whole or particular services, and the output: what is achieved as a result of the activity being carried out. For example, the establishment of an enquiry service for users requires the input of staff, materials, equipment and floor space. The output is the number of enquiries received, the number satisfied, the level of use made of the resources and the use of other services, for example, the reservation service, arising from the original activity. These measures can then be compared each year to see if the effectiveness of the library service is improving.

▶ The Danish National Library Authority provides public libraries in Denmark with a database, computer software and a guidebook for performance measurement. It gives the opportunity for all public libraries in Denmark to collect information in the same way, which gives them an excellent tool for bench-marking. They are also able to compare the statistics with the results of a major user survey (**http://www. kib.dk**).

▶ A system of participative management for public libraries has been developed in Chile. It operates by studying the surrounding environment and the community and providing procedures for the design, planning and realization of cultural activities with the participation of local people. It includes procedures for following up the participative management, measuring the quality of the work and the impact that public libraries are having on the local community.

Computer technology makes performance measurement a simpler task and enables sophisticated models of library use to be established and used in service development. Performance measurement should be a planned process carried out with consistency over a period of time. Further information about library performance indicators can be found in ISO 11620:1998 *Information and documentation. Library performance indicators.*

Another way of gaining a useful indication of the success of a library service is to compare key input and output measurements with other public libraries of similar size and characteristics. This is usually known as benchmarking and is a useful adjunct to performance measurements carried out internally.

6.11   Marketing and promotion

Library managers can use marketing techniques to enable them to understand the needs of their users and to plan effectively to meet those needs. The library should also promote its services to the public to ensure that they are kept informed of the services provided to meet their library and information requirements.

6.11.1 Marketing and promotion policy

The library should have a written communications, marketing and promo-
tions policy to enable it to undertake a planned promotion of its services
to the public. The policy should include a marketing and communication
strategy and methods of evaluating promotional programmes.

6.11.2 Marketing and promotion plan

To enable the library to achieve its marketing strategy, a coherent marketing and promotion plan should be developed based on the agreed policy.
It could include the following elements:

- making positive use of print, electronic and communications media
- displays and exhibits
- effective interior and exterior sign-posting
- regular publications and the preparation of resource lists and pamphlets
- reading and literacy campaigns
- designing campaigns to meet the needs of people with physical and sensory disabilities
- book fairs
- library websites
- links to and from related websites and portals
- friends of the library groups
- annual library week celebrations and other collective promotional
  activities
- special years of celebration and anniversaries
- library listings in the telephone book and other community directories
- fund-raising activities and campaigns
- public-speaking activities and liaison with community groups
- special library publications, e.g., history of the library, history of the
  community.

This list is not exhaustive and other elements can be added depending on
local circumstances.

6.11.3 Working with the media

Library staff should be trained to use communication media to promote the library service and respond to media enquiries. They should be able to write articles for local newspapers and prepare press releases. They should be familiar with the techniques of speaking and being interviewed on radio and television. They should also be able to promote the library and its services via computer and telecommunication networks including the creation of library websites.

6.11.4 Community support

The library managers must ensure that the community is aware of the importance of the library service. Municipal, regional and national funding bodies should be made fully aware of the important place that the library occupies in the community, and support its development.

6.11.5 Gaining community support

The library should have an agreed policy and a sustained programme for developing community support. This can include:

- maintaining a 'friends of the library' organization for fund-raising and general support
- working with community advocates in support of major initiatives such as new buildings and services
- forming liaisons with community groups to enhance parts of the collection or strengthen specific services
- working with groups that wish to speak out on behalf of the library service and its development
- participation by library staff in activities aimed at increasing awareness of the variety and value of the library service.

The support of the community also depends on the library delivering the services it has promised to deliver.

6.11.6 Advocacy

The library should have established and adopted written policies that define its role in generating public support for the library service.

A well informed public can provide valuable support for the public library service and actively promote it within the community. Getting people to talk positively about the library and its services is one of the most effective marketing tools. Lobbying involves interaction with decision-makers to secure specific objectives at an appropriate point in the legislative, policy-making or budget process.

6.11.7 Working with governing bodies

Library managers should meet at least annually with the library's principal governing and funding body to review the library's services, development plans, achievements and obstacles. Librarians should look for as many opportunities as possible to involve its governing body in its major activities. Events such as the opening of a new library, the launching of a service, the installation of public Internet access, the opening of a new collection and the inauguration of a fund-raising drive can be used for this purpose.

6.11.8 Participation in community life

One of the most effective promotional strategies is the participation of well-informed library staff and committee or board members in community activities. Examples include:

- presenting book and activity reviews on radio and television
- working with adults and children's literature and cultural groups
- writing a newspaper column
- supporting literacy organizations and campaigns
- participating in the activities of local organizations
- assisting with school-based initiatives
- participating in local history and genealogy societies
- being a member of a service organization, e.g., Rotary
- visiting local organizations to promote the library service.

6.11.9 Evaluation

The library should carry out a regular evaluation of its marketing and promotion programme and ensure the results of the evaluation are taken into account when planning future programmes.

The IFLA/UNESCO Public Library Manifesto

A Gateway to Knowledge

Freedom, prosperity and the development of society and of individuals are fundamental human values. They will only be attained through the ability of well-informed citizens to exercise their democratic rights and to play an active role in society. Constructive participation and the development of democracy depend on satisfactory education as well as on free and unlimited access to knowledge, thought, culture and information.

The public library, the local gateway to knowledge, provides a basic condition for lifelong learning, independent decision-making and cultural development of the individual and social groups.

This Manifesto proclaims UNESCO's belief in the public library as a living force for education, culture and information, and as an essential agent for the fostering of peace and spiritual welfare through the minds of men and women.

UNESCO therefore encourages national and local governments to support and actively engage in the development of public libraries.

The Public Library

The public library is the local centre of information, making all kinds of knowledge and information readily available to its users.

The services of the public library are provided on the basis of equality of access for all, regardless of age, race, sex, religion, nationality, language or social status. Specific services and materials must be provided for those users who cannot, for whatever reason, use the regular services and materials, for example linguistic minorities, people with disabilities or people in hospital or prison.

All age groups must find material relevant to their needs. Collections and services have to include all types of appropriate media and modern technologies as well as traditional materials. High quality and relevance to local needs and conditions are fundamental. Material must reflect current trends and the evolution of society, as well as the memory of human endeavour and imagination.

Collections and services should not be subject to any form of ideological, political or religious censorship, nor commercial pressures.

Missions of the Public Library

Missions of the public library. The following key missions which relate to information, literacy, education and culture should be at the core of public library services:

1 creating and strengthening reading habits in children from an early age;
2 supporting both individual and self conducted education as well as formal education at all levels;
3 providing opportunities for personal creative development;
4 stimulating the imagination and creativity of children and young people;
5 promoting awareness of cultural heritage, appreciation of the arts, scientific achievements and innovations;
6 providing access to cultural expressions of all performing arts;
7 fostering inter-cultural dialogue and favouring cultural diversity;
8 supporting the oral tradition;
9 ensuring access for citizens to all sorts of community information;
10 providing adequate information services to local enterprises, associations and interest groups;
11 facilitating the development of information and computer literacy skills;
12 supporting and participating in literary activities and programmes for all age groups, and initiating such activities if necessary.

Funding, legislation and networks

The public library shall in principle be free of charge. The public library is the responsibility of local and national authorities. It must be supported by specific legislation and financed by national and local government. It has to be an essential component of any long-term strategy for culture, information provision, literacy and education.

To ensure nationwide library coordination and cooperation, legislation and strategic plans must also define and promote a national library network based on agreed standards of service

The public library network must be designed in relation to national, regional, research and special libraries as well as libraries in schools, colleges and universities.

Operation and management

A clear policy must be formulated, defining objectives, priorities and services in relation to the local community needs. The public library has to be organized effectively and professional standards of operation must be maintained.

Cooperation with relevant partners-for example, user groups and other professionals at local, regional, national as well as international level-has to be ensured.

Services have to be physically accessible to all members of the community. This requires well situated library buildings, good reading and study facilities, as well as relevant technologies and sufficient opening hours convenient to the users. It equally implies outreach services for those unable to visit the library.

The library services must be adapted to the different needs of communities in rural and urban areas.

The librarian is an active intermediary between users and resources. Professional and continuing education of the librarian is indispensable to ensure adequate services.

Outreach and user education programmes have to be provided to help users benefit from all the resources.

Implementing the Manifesto

Decision makers at national and local levels and the library community at large, around the world, are hereby urged to implement the principles expressed in this Manifesto.

This Manifesto is prepared in cooperation with the International Federation of Library Associations and Institutions (IFLA).

The Manifesto can be seen in over twenty languages on the IFLA website: http://www.ifla.org/VII/s8/unesco/manif.htm

The Finnish Library Act (904/1998)

Issued in Helsinki on the 4th of December 1998
In accordance with a decision of Parliament the following is enacted

Chapter 1 Objectives

1. This act prescribes the library and information services to be provided by municipal public libraries, and the promotion of these services both nationally and regionally.

2. The objective of the library and information services provided by public libraries is to promote equal opportunities among citizens for personal cultivation, for literary and cultural pursuits, for continuous development of knowledge, personal skills and civic skills, for internationalisation, and for lifelong learning.

Library activities also aim at promoting the development of virtual and interactive network services and their educational and cultural contents.

Chapter 2 Arranging library and information services

3. The municipality shall be responsible for arranging the library and information services referred to in this act.

The municipality may provide the library and information services independently, or partly or totally in co-operation with other municipalities, or in any other way. The municipality is responsible for the services being in accordance with this act.

Library users shall have access to library and information professionals, and to continually renewing library material and equipment.

In a bilingual municipality, the needs of both language groups shall be taken into consideration on equal grounds

In the municipalities of the Saami home area, the needs of both the Saami and the Finnish language groups shall be taken into consideration on equal grounds.

Chapter 3 The library and information service network

4. A public library shall operate in co-operation with other public libraries, with research libraries and with libraries in educational establishments, as part of the national and international networks of library and information services.

The libraries acting as the central library for public libraries and as provincial libraries supplement the services of public libraries.

The central library for public libraries is a public library in a municipality appointed by the relevant ministry, with the consent of the municipality. Its sphere of operations shall be the whole country.

A provincial library is a public library in a municipality appointed by the relevant ministry, with the consent of the municipality. The sphere of operations shall be laid down by the relevant ministry.

The tasks of the central library and the provincial library shall be enacted in a decree. The relevant ministry can, after consulting the municipality, cancel the designation as central or a provincial library.

Chapter 4 Library services free of charge

5. The use of the library's own collections within the library and borrowing from them shall be free of charge.

Inter-library loans issued by the central library and by the provincial libraries to public libraries shall be free of charge.

For other library transactions, the municipality may charge a fee amounting to the prime cost of the transaction at most.

For a specific reason, the fee which would otherwise be fixed to amount to the prime cost may exceed this.

Chapter 5 Evaluation

6. The municipality shall evaluate the library and information service it provides.

The purpose of the evaluation is to improve access to library and information services and to promote their development. The evaluation shall monitor the implementation of the library and information services and the quality and cost-effectiveness of the services.

Each municipality is obliged to take part in evaluation referred to by this clause.

Decisions about national evaluation and about national participation in international evaluations shall be made by the relevant ministry, which shall carry out the evaluation together with the Provincial State Offices. The municipality shall contribute to the evaluation referred to in this subsection.

Salient findings of the evaluation shall be made public.

Chapter 6 State administration of library and information services

7 The relevant ministry shall be the national administrative for library and information services. The provincial state office shall be the regional administrative authority. The tasks of the provincial state office shall be enacted in a decree.

Chapter 7 Miscellaneous regulations

8. The library system shall have a sufficient number of staff qualified for library and information service and other personnel.

The qualification requirements for library staff shall be enacted in a decree.

For a specific reason, the relevant ministry may grant exception from the formal qualification requirements.

9. The municipality shall receive statutory state aid towards the cost of operating the library under the Act on the Financing of Educational and Cultural Provision (635/1998).

The municipality shall receive a government grant towards the costs of constructing and renovating a library under the Act on the Financing of Educational and Cultural Provision. The purchase of a mobile library bus or boat shall also be regarded as construction.

10. The library may issue library rules which contain provisions concerning the use of the library and the rights and duties of the library user. Infringement of the library rules shall be chargeable with fines commensurate with the infringement.

11. More detailed provisions on the application of this act shall be issued by statute.

THE FINNISH LIBRARY DECREE (1078/998)

Issued at Helsinki on 18th December 1998

Section 1 Functions of the Central Library of Public Libraries

The central library of public libraries shall

1. act as the national interlibrary lending centre
2. promote co-operation of public libraries and between public and scientific libraries
3. develop common methods and instruments necessary for organising library and information services
4. perform other duties assigned by the competent Ministry.

Section 2 Functions of a Provincial Library

A Provincial Library shall

1. support the information and interlibrary lending services of the public libraries within its region
2. develop information services relating to its own sphere of operation
3. provide the personnel of the sphere of operation with training in new forms and development projects of library work
4. perform other duties assigned by the competent Ministry.

Section 3 Functions of the State Provincial Office

The State Provincial Office shall

1. in co-operation with the competent Ministry, monitor and promote library and information services needed by the population, and evaluate the accessibility and quality of the services
2. promote regional, national and international development projects in the field of library and information service
3. perform other duties assigned by the competent Ministry.

Section 4 Qualification Requirements

A minimum of two thirds of the personnel referred to in Section 8, Subsection 1 of the Library Act (904/1998), must have a university degree, or college diploma, or a vocational qualification which includes, or has been supplemented with, a minimum of 20 credits of library and information studies at a university or a vocational institution.

The qualification required from the person responsible for the library and information services in a municipality shall be a higher university degree which includes, or has been supplemented with, a minimum of 35 credits of library and information studies.

Section 5 Entry into Force

The Decree shall come into force on the first day of January 1999.

The provisions of Section 4, Subsection 1 shall not apply to the personnel employed by a library at the time when this Decree comes into force.

Any process of filling a vacant post or position pending at the time when this Decree comes into force shall be subject to / comply with the qualification requirements valid prior to the entry into force of this Decree

Before the entry into force of this Decree, necessary measures may be taken to implement it.

Section 6 Transitional Provisions concerning Personnel

Not detailed here

Section 7 Transitional Provisions concerning the Completion of Studies

Not detailed here

Appendix 3

Customer charter

A number of public library services have prepared customer/user charters. The following example is from Buckinghamshire County Library, England.

Buckinghamshire County Library
Library Service Customer Charter

We want library users in Buckinghamshire to receive a high quality service. This Charter sets out the standards we aim to achieve in all our libraries, and which you have a right to expect. It also tells you what to do if you want our service to change or improve.

Our library promise

- We have a network of branch and mobile libraries throughout Buckinghamshire. We will consult local people to ensure that as far as possible opening times reflect the need of their communities.
- Our computer catalogues will provide customers in every branch with details of the complete range of library service stock.
- Items borrowed can be returned or renewed at any one of our libraries, not just the one they were borrowed from.

Our promise of service

- You will be served by staff wearing identity badges, who have received training in customer care.
- Our staff will be helpful and courteous, and have the skills and experience to do their jobs well.

- You will not normally have to wait longer than 3 minutes to be served at a counter or enquiry desk, except at peak periods.
- We will provide an answer to your enquiries while you wait, or advise you how long this will take.
- We will answer your letters and telephone calls promptly and efficiently, and reply or acknowledge within 3 working days. If necessary, a full reply will follow within 10 working days.
- We will supply 70% of requested items within 15 days and 80% within 30 days. There may be a longer wait for very popular items, or those obtained from outside the county. We will let you know about the progress of your request whenever you ask us.

Our promise on access and equality

- We will provide services that reflect the cultural and linguistic diversity of local communities.
- We will make every effort to provide facilities and services that are accessible to people with disabilities.
- We will provide a library service to meet the needs of special client groups, including the housebound and those in residential care.
- We will give appropriate advice and training to enable our staff to meet the needs of all our customers, without discrimination.

Our promise to listen and consult

- We will provide more information about our services whenever you need it.
- We will listen to your views about the library service. If you have any comments or opinions you would like to share with us, talk to your local library manager or fill in a Comments, Complaints and Compliments form.
- We will carry out a full customer satisfaction survey in every library at least every three years, and publish the results.
- We will consult our customers on major issues affecting the service, and keep you informed about changes and developments.

Our performance against the promises in this charter will be closely monitored. Our standards will be reviewed each year and the results published.

Library Building Standards – Ontario, Canada and Barcelona, Spain

There is no universal standard of measurement for public library buildings. However standards have been developed in some countries or regions. As examples, which may be useful when planning a library building, standards used by Ontario, Canada and Barcelona, Spain are included in this appendix. It is important that the unique needs of any community must be a primary factor in determining the final space allocated for the library. The examples in this appendix should be used in conjunction with all the sections of Paragraph 3.10 Library Buildings.

Library planners should keep in mind that automation has changed library services patterns and the design and size of the library must take current and future technology into account.

Ontario Public Library Guidelines 1997

The following methods are used by Ontario Public Libraries to determine floor-space requirements.

1. **Average square feet per capita.** For a community under 100 000 population the appropriate standard is 56 sq. m. (600 sq. ft.) per 1000 capita.
2. **Building size determined by major components.**
(1) Collection space: Collection space can be determined by using the average standard of 110 volumes per sq. m. (10.8 sq. ft.) This allows for low shelving and wider aisles in specialized areas such as children's and ref-

erence collections, with regular shelving and aisle allocations in the larger non-fiction area.

Space required = 1 sq. m. (10.8 sq. ft.) for every 110 volumes.

(2) User space: A acceptable standard for user space in a library is 5 user spaces
per 1000 capita. This allows for individual study stations in adult and children's areas, as well as informal seating, reference tables, A/V stations, public Internet stations.

A space of 2.8 sq. m. (30 sq. ft.) for each reader station is an acceptable
standard.

(3) Staff space: A recommended library standard used to determine the
number of staff is 1 staff member per 2000 population (See also Paragraph
5.6). Staff space can be determined by using a total space per staff member of 16.3 sq. m. (175 sq. ft.) This figure includes work-stations, reader
services desks, circulation areas, lounge, locker facilities, etc.

Space required: 16.3 sq. m. (175 sq. ft.) per staff member @ 1 staff member per 2000 population.

(4) Multi-purpose rooms: Each library should assign space for these rooms
based on community service and programme objectives.

(5) Non-assignable space: Non-assignable space includes washrooms, janito-
rial space, mechanical, elevators, staircases, etc. The need for non-assignable space is reduced where the library shares washrooms, mechanical areas
etc. with another tenant in one building.

Space required = 20% of net space (i.e. 20% of the total of items (1) to
(4)).

(6) Minimum overall size
The minimum size for an independent library should not be less than
370 sq. m. (4000 sq. ft.).

In a multi-branch system, the branch should have not less than 230 sq. m. (2500 sq. ft.) of floor space plus 14 sq. m. (150 sq. ft.) for each additional 1000 volumes over 3000 volumes in its collection.

Ontario Public Library Guidelines: a development tool for small, medium and country libraries, Sudbury, Ontario, Ontario Library Service North, 1997.

Diputació de Barcelona Library Service: Basic Public Library Standards Revised March 1999

	Branch Library	Public Library			Central Library		County Library	
Pop.	Towns 3000–5000	Towns 5000–10 000	Towns 10–20 000	Towns 20–30 000	Towns 30–50 000	Towns over 50 000	Towns up to 50 000	Towns over 50 000
PREMISES, m²								
Public Areas								
Lobby	15–15	15–30	30–40	40–60	60–110	110–150	60–110	110–150
Multi-purpose Hall	–50	50–60	60–80	80–100	100–150	150–200	100–150	150–200
General Area: Lending / Reference	130–200	200–270	270–410	410–645	645–930	930–1450	580–930	930–1450
Magazines / Audiovisuals	60–90	90–100	100–115	115–140	140–250	250–400	110–250	250–400
Children's Area	60–90	90–120	120–160	160–225	225–300	300–360	180–300	300–360
Areas Reserved for Staff								
Office	15–15	15–20	20–20	20–30	30–40	40–100	50–65	65–180
Storeroom	20–30	30–40	40–60	60–80	80–150	150–230	115–210	210–350
Rest Area	–10	10–10	10–15	15–20	20–30	30–35	20–35	35–40
Car Park					–40	40–75	75–150	150–170
Programme Area	300–500	500–650	650–900	900–1300	1300–2000	2000–3000	1300–2200	2200–3300
Service Areas								
Cleaning Facilities								
Corridors, etc.		The total built area is the programme area plus 30%						
Toilet Facilities								
Total Built Area	390–650	650–845	845–1170	1170–1690	1690–2600	2600–3900	1690–2860	2860–4290
FACILITIES								
Places for Reading, Audiovisuals and Computer Work (number of places)								
General Area	20–30	30–40	40–60	60–85	85–115	115–145	50–115	115–145
Children's Area	15–20	20–25	25–35	35–50	50–65	65–75	40–65	65–75
Magazines: Table	2–4	4–4	4–6	6–10	10–15	15–20	6–15	15–20
Informal	6–8	8–10	10–10	10–15	15–20	20–25	10–20	20–25
Audiovisuals	4	6–8	8–12	12–16	16–20	20–25	16–20	20–25
PCs – General	4	6–8	8–10	10–14	14–18	18–27	14–18	18–27
PCs – CD-ROM		1–2	2–2	2–4	4–5	5–9	5–6	6–9
Multi-purpose Hall	–35	35–45	45–60	60–75	75–115	115–150	75–115	115–150
Shelf Space: 33 books x m	300	395–760	760–1090	1090–1515	1515–2120	2120–2725	1820–2425	2425–3335
CD Racks: 225 CD/60x90 cm unit		5–7	7–10	10–13	13–17	17–25	15–20	20–30

Resource list

General

An Chomhairle Leabharlanna (The Library Council), *Joining forces: delivering libraries and information services in the information age*, Dublin, The Library Council, 2000.

Associazione Italiana Biblioteche, *Linee guida per la valutazione delle biblioteche pubbliche Italiane*, Rome, Associazione Italiana Biblioteche, 2000.

Baró i Llambias, M and Mañà i Terré, T., *Formar-se per informar-se: propostes per a la integració de la biblioteca a l'escola*, Barcelona, Edicions 62, Rosa Sensat, 1994.

Benton Foundation, *Buildings, books and bytes: libraries and communities in the digital age*, published by the Benton Foundation at the request of the W. K. Kellogg Foundation, 1996.
http://www.benton.org/Library/Kellogg/buildings.html

Benton Foundation, *Local places, global connections: libraries in the digital age*, published by the Benton Foundation and Libraries for the Future, 1999.
http://www.benton.org/Library/Libraries/home.html

Bibliotheken '93. Strukturen - Aufgaben - Positionen, Bundesvereinigung Deutscher Bibliotheksverbände (BDB), Berlin, Goettingen, BDB, Berlin, Deutsches Bibliotheksinstitut, 1994.

Calenge, Bertrand, *Les petites bibliothèques*, Paris, Cercle de la librarie, 1993.

Council for Cultural Co-operation, Culture Committee, *Council of Europe/EBLIDA guidelines on library legislation and policy in Europe*, 2000.

Domínguez Sanjurjo, María Ramona, *Nuevas formas de organización y servicios en la biblioteca pública*, Gijón, Spain, Trea, 1997.

England. Culture, Media and Sport Committee (UK), *Culture, Media and Sport - sixth report - public libraries*, London, House of Commons, 2000. **http://www.parliament.the-stationery-office.co.uk/pa/cm199900/ cmselect/cmcumeds/241/24102.htm**

England. Department of Culture, Media and Sport, *Comprehensive, efficient and modern public libraries - standards and assessment*, London, Department of Culture, Media and Sport, 2001.

England. Libraries, Information and Archives Division, *Libraries for all: social inclusion in public libraries: policy guidelines for local authorities in England*, London, Department for Culture, Media and Sport, 1999.

England, Library and Information Commission, *New library: the people's network*, London, Department for Culture, Media and Sport, 1998.

Finland. Ministry of Education, *Public libraries in Finland - gateways to knowledge and culture*, Helsinki, Ministry of Education, 1999. **http://www.minedu.fi/minedu/culture/libraries_gateways.html**

Firsov, V. R., *Gosudarstvennoye zakonodatelnoye regulirovanie dejatelnosti bibliotek*, St Petersburg, Rossijskaja natsional naja biblioteka, 2000.

Florida Library Association, *Standards for Florida public libraries: a vision for the 21st century*, Florida, Florida Library Association, 1995. **http://www.dos.state.fl.us/dlis/Standards/index.html**

Germany. Working Party Joint Career Profile of the BDB, *Career profile 2000: the changing roles of libraries and librarians*, Berlin, Bundesvereinigung Deutscher Bibliotheksverbände eV, 2000. **http://www.bdbverband.de/index2.html**

Greenhalgh, Liz and Worpole, Ken with Landry, Charles, *Libraries in a world of cultural change*, London, UCL Press, 1995.

Hayes, Robert M. and Walter, Virginia A., *Strategic management for public libraries: a handbook*, Westport, Conn., Greenwood Press, 1996.

Himmel, Ethel and Wilson, William James, with the ReVision Committee of the Public Library Association, *Planning for results: a public library transformation process - the guidebook*, Chicago, American Library Association, 1998.

Himmel, Ethel and Wilson, William James, with the ReVision Committee of the Public Library Association, *Planning for results: a public library transformation process - the how-to manual*, Chicago, American Library Association, 1998.

IER Planning, Research and Management Services, *The library's contribution to your community: a resource manual for libraries to document their social and economic contribution to the local community*, Gloucester, Ontario, Canada, Southern Ontario Library Service, 1998.

Illinois Library Association, *Serving our public: standards for Illinois public libraries*, Chicago, Illinois Library Association, 1997.

Information Centre for Information Ethics
http://www.infoethics.net

Information on guidelines and standards in Spain
http://www.fundaciongsr.es/documentos/default3.htm

Information on library law in Spain
http://www.mcu.es/legislacion/i_legislac.html

Ireland. Department of Environment and Local Government, *Branching out: a new public library service*, Dublin, Stationery Office, 1998.

ISO 11620, *Information and documentation. Library performance indicators*, Geneva, ISO, 1998.

King Research Ltd, *Keys to success: performance indicators for public libraries: a manual of performance measures and indicators*, London, HMSO, 1998.

Kulicova, L. V., *Publichnaja biblioteka v uslovijah mestnogo samoupravlenija, Posobie*, St Petersburg, Rossijskaja natsionalnaja biblioteka, 2000.

La biblioteca escolar en el contexto de la reforma educativa: documento marco, Madrid, Ministerio de Educación y Ciencia, 1995.

La biblioteca pública, un compromiso político: primeras jornados "Biblioteca pública y políticas culturales", Barcelona, Fundación Bertelsmann, 1997.

Library Association, *Code of professional conduct and guidance notes*, 3rd edn, London, The Library Association, 1999.

Library Association, *Model statement of standards for public library services*, London, The Library Association, 1995.

Library Association, Public Library Charter Working group, *A charter for public libraries*, London, The Library Association, 1993.

Library Board of Queensland, *Guidelines and standards for Queensland public libraries*, Brisbane, Library Board of Queensland, 1997.

McClure, Charles R., et al., *Planning and role setting for public libraries: a manual of options and procedures*, Chicago, American Library Association, 1987.

Le métier de bibliothécaire, Paris, Cercle de la librarie, 1996.

Modelnij standart dejatelnosti publichnoj biblioteki, Proekt 9 vinositsja na obsugdenie Sektsiej po bibliotechnoj politike i zakonodatel stvu RBA, St Petersburg, 2000.

Moore, Nick, *Measuring the performance of public libraries,* Paris, UNESCO, 1989.

Ontario Library Service North, *Ontario public library guidelines: a development tool for small, medium and county libraries,* Sudbury, Ontario, Canada, Ontario Library Service North, 1997 (with updates to June 2000).

Oregon Library Association, *Standards for Oregon public libraries 2000.* **http://www.olaweb.org/pld/standards.html**

Ot massovoj k publichnoj biblioteke, Materiali seminara (10–11 Nojabrja 1992 Moskva), Moscow, 1993.

Performance measurement and quality management in public libraries, Proceedings of IFLA Satellite Meeting, Berlin, 25–28 August 1997, Berlin, Deutsche Bibliothekinstitut, 1998.

Rural information provision in developing countries: measuring performance and impact, prepared for UNESCO on behalf of IFLA by Antoinette F. Correa, Kingo J. Mchombu, Djibril Ndiaye, Gloria M. Rodriguez, Diana Rosenberg and N. U. Yapa, Paris, UNESCO, 1997. **http://www.unesco.org/webworld/highlights/rural_250399.html**

Salaberria, Ramon, *Bibliotecas públicas y bibliotecas escolares: una colaboración imprescindible,* Madrid, Ministerio de Educación y Cultura, 1997.

Scotland. Convention of Scottish Local Authorities, *Standards for public library services in Scotland: a report by a working party appointed by the Arts and Recreation Committee of the Convention of Scottish Local Authorities,* Edinburgh, Convention of Scottish Local Authorities, 1995.

Singapore. Library 2000 Review Committee, *Investing in a learning nation: report of the Library 2000 Review Committee,* Singapore, SNP Publishers, 2000.

Sturges, Paul and Neill, Richard, *The quiet struggle: information and libraries for the people of Africa,* 2nd edn, Mansell, London, 1998.

Taesch-Wahlen, Danielle, *Concevoir, réaliser et organiser une bibliothèque: mémento à l'usage des élus, des responsables administratifs et des bibliothécaires,* Paris, Cercle de la librairie, 1997.

Texas Library Association, Public Libraries Division, Standards Committee, *Guidelines for Texas public libraries,* Austin, Texas, Texas Library Association, 1992.

Turner, Bridget, *Research document of the lack of study facilities in Gauteng Province and its impact on community libraries*, Gauteng Provincial Library and Information Services, South Africa, 1999.

Wisconsin Department of Public Instruction, *Wisconsin public library standards*, 3rd edn, Madison, Wisconsin, State of Wisconsin Department of Public Instruction, Public Library Development, 2000.
http://www.dpi.state.wi.us/dlcl/pld/standard.html

Zweig, Douglas, Wilcox Johnson, Debra, Robbins, Jane, et al., *The TELL IT! manual: the complete program for evaluating library performance*, Chicago, American Library Association, 1996.

Buildings

Brawner, Lee B., and Beck, Donald K. Jr, *Determining your public library's future size: a needs assessment and planning model*, Chicago, American Library Association, 1996.

Dahlgren, Anders, *Planning the small library facility*, 2nd edn, Small Libraries Publication, #23, Chicago and London, Library Administration and Management Association, 1996.

Dahlgren, Anders, *Public library space needs: a planning guide, 1998*, State of Wisconsin, Department of Public Instruction, Public Library Development, 1998.
http://www.dpi.state.wi.us/dlcl/pld/plspace.html

IFLA Section on Library Buildings and Equipment, *Intelligent library buildings: proceedings of the tenth seminar of the IFLA Section on Library Buildings and Equipment, The Hague, Netherlands, 24-29 August, 1997*, Marie-Françoise Bisbrouck and Marc Chauveinc (eds), IFLA Publication - 88, Munich, K. G. Saur, 1999.

Koontz, Christine M., *Library facility siting and location handbook*, Westport, Conn., Greenwood Press, 1997.

McCabe, Gerard, *Planning for a new generation of public library buildings*, Westport, Conn., Greenwood Press, 2000.

Prototipo de bibliotecas públicas, Madrid, Ministerio de Cultura, 1995.

Sannwald, William W., *Checklist of library building design considerations*, 3rd edn, Chicago, American Library Association, 1997.

IFLA/UNESCO manifestos

IFLA, Section of Public Libraries, *The IFLA/UNESCO Public Library Manifesto*, The Hague, IFLA, 1995. Available in various languages at: **http://www.ifla.org/VII/s8/unesco/manif.htm**

IFLA, *The IFLA/UNESCO School Library Manifesto*, Ottawa, National Library of Canada, 1999.

IFLA standards and guidelines

IFLA, Mobile Libraries Round Table, *Mobile library guidelines*, Professional Report #28, By Robert Pestell, The Hague, IFLA, 1991.

IFLA, Section of Libraries for the Blind, Standards Development Committee, *Approved recommendations on working out national standards of library services for the blind*, F. Cylke, W. Byrne, H. Fiddler, S.S. Zharkov (eds), The Hague, IFLA, 1983.

IFLA, Section for Libraries for Children and Young Adults, *Guidelines for library services for young adults*, The Hague, IFLA, (n.d.).

IFLA, Section for Libraries Serving Disadvantaged Persons, *Guidelines for library services to deaf people*, 2nd edn, Professional Report # 62, By John Michael Day, The Hague, IFLA, 2000 [also available in French, German, Russian and Spanish].

IFLA, Section for Libraries Serving Disadvantaged Persons, *Guidelines for library services to prisoners*, Professional Report # 34, Frances E. Kaiser (ed.), The Hague, IFLA, 1995 [also available in German].

IFLA, Section for Libraries Serving Disadvantaged Persons, *Guidelines for libraries serving hospital patients and the elderly and disabled in long-term care facilities*, Professional Report #61, The Hague, IFLA, 2000.

IFLA, Section for Library Services to Multicultural Populations, *Multicultural communities: guidelines for library services*, 2nd edn, The Hague, IFLA, 1998 [also available in French and Spanish].

IFLA, Section of Public Libraries, *The public library as the gateway to the information society: the revision of the IFLA guidelines for public libraries, proceedings of the IFLA/UNESCO Pre-Conference Seminar on Public Libraries, 1997*, The Hague, IFLA, 1998.

IFLA, Section of Public Libraries: website of public library acts (various) **http://www.ifla.org/V/cdoc/acts.htm**

IFLA, Working Group, *Guidelines for libraries serving hospital patients and disabled people in the community*, Professional Report #2, The Hague, IFLA, 1984.

IFLA guidelines under development, February 2001

IFLA, Section of Libraries for the Blind, *National standards of library services for the blind* [anticipated publication date 2002].

IFLA, Section of Libraries for Children and Young Adults, *Guidelines for children's services* [anticipated publication date 2002].

IFLA, Section of Libraries for Disadvantaged Persons, *Guidelines for dyslexia* [anticipated publication date 2001].

IFLA, Section of School Libraries and Resource Centres, *Guidelines for school libraries* [anticipated publication date 2002].

Index